A CLASSROOM OF HER OWN

For my mother and father,
my finest teachers

A Classroom of Her Own

How New Teachers Develop Instructional, Professional, and Cultural Competence

Dana Haight Cattani

CORWIN PRESS, INC.
A Sage Publications Company
Thousand Oaks, California

For information:

Corwin Press, Inc.
A Sage Publications Company
2455 Teller Road
Thousand Oaks, California 91320
www.corwinpress.com

Sage Publications Ltd.
6 Bonhill Street
London EC2A 4PU
United Kingdom

Sage Publications India Pvt. Ltd.
M-32 Market
Greater Kailash I
New Delhi 110 048 India

Printed in the United States of America

Library of Congress Cataloging-in-Publication Data

Cattani, Dana Haight.
  A classroom of her own: How new teachers develop instructional, professional, and cultural competence / by Dana Haight Cattani.
      p. cm.
Includes bibliographical references and index.
  ISBN 0-7619-4569-5 (c) — ISBN 0-7619-4570-9 (p)
  1. First year teachers—United States—Case studies. 2. Women teachers—United States—Case studies. I. Title.
  LB2844.1.N4 C38 2002
  371.1'0082—dc21

                                                    2002000050

This book is printed on acid-free paper.

02 03 04 05 06 07 7 6 5 4 3 2 1

Acquisitions Editor: Faye Zucker
Editorial Assistant: Julia Parnell
Production Editor: Olivia Weber
Typesetter: Rebecca Evans
Copy Editor: Kristin Bergstad
Cover Designer: Michael Dubowe
Cover Photographer: Michael Dubowe
Production Artist: Sandra Ng

Contents

Sidebar Directory

Tips for Administrators and Mentors

Foreword

This book is a commentary on becoming a teacher. It is a set of thoughtful essays based on observations of a group of young, white, middle-class, female teachers learning what it means to be alone at the head of a classroom. Before the tyranny of prose and propriety triumphed over alliteration and alacrity, the title was *Chicks in Charge*. The teachers are similar in age, ethnicity, class, and gender, not only to each other but also to a clear majority of new teachers in the United States. They find themselves in classrooms facing similar problems and experiencing similar doubts.

With lovely detail and empathic understanding, Cattani paints a textured picture of the development of competence. The picture is organized around the complications of ordinary life in a classroom for these new teachers. They have had little experience with exercising authority and are not sure how to do it. They have to learn how to act as teachers—how to speak, how to dress, how to think, how to manage themselves and their classrooms, how to confront their emotions, how to deal with parents and administrators, how to react to a role and to situations that are different in important ways from what they expected and from what their experience had been.

It is hard to read the story of these teachers without being struck both by the curiosity of a world that assigns naïve novices to positions of authority and responsibility and by the persistence, imagination, and fortitude of these young women. They floundered, but they recovered. Misleadingly recruited, inadequately prepared, poorly equipped, and frequently unaided, they survived. At moments, they thrived. They managed to make it through each day and gradually became professionals. Like all good morality tales, the book describes a life filled with struggles, victories, defeats, and lessons.

Cattani is a good observer, and she reports the actions, feelings, confusions, frustrations, and successes of the teachers with acute sensitivity. In a careful and sympathetic way, she has created an ethnographic sketch of what it is like to be a new teacher. The book, however, is not just a portrayal of the work lives of these women. It is a commentary, a kind of primer for others in similar circumstances. Thus, it combines description with prescription, with suggestions for other young, white, middle-class women who wake up one morning to find themselves in charge of a classroom. Both in her description and in her advice, Cattani has crafted a book that new teachers can read and from which they can take wisdom and heart.

The reader should be warned, however, that there is a deceptive simplicity about the book, both in its descriptions and in its advice. The descriptions are understated; the advice is soft-spoken. It avoids pretense and elaborate language. Like all good descriptions and good advice, the chapters achieve useful meaning particularly through their links to the concrete stories of the teachers' lives, not through big words or elaborate theories. The ideas sneak up on you, artfully concealed in practical suggestions and simple declarative sentences.

The biggest deception, however, is in tempting the reader to think the book is only about teachers. Despite the careful attention to a set of specific concrete situations in schools and to the ways in which understanding the dynamics of those contexts is essential to understanding teachers, the book has lessons that extend beyond the relatively narrow frame of its focus. It illuminates, for example, the problems of other parts of the school system, particularly parallel problems in the recruitment and training of administrators.

Moreover, the lessons of the book are relevant to thinking about a large class of organizational personnel problems that occur in business, government, churches, and military organizations. The recruitment and training of individuals for jobs is often poorly tuned to the demands of the jobs. During the period from 1940 to 1944, for example, the U.S. Army grew enormously as the country mobilized to fight the Second World War. The army trained rapidly and put into place in battle a very large number of junior officers, young men who had, for the most part, neither previous military nor leadership experience. Many of these young officers died. The casualty rate among second lieutenants was high. Many of them distinguished themselves. Many of them survived.

The survivors told a consistent story. They were not prepared. They had little experience with exercising authority and were not sure how to do it. They had to learn how to act as officers—how to speak, how to dress, how to think, how to manage themselves and their units, how to confront their emotions, how to deal with outsiders and superiors, how to react to a role and to situations that were different in important ways from what they had expected and from what their experience had been. They would never forget the experience, neither the terror of it nor the sense of triumph at having survived it.

Dana Cattani's story is remarkably similar. Hers is a story not of young men but of young women, not of finding oneself in the unfamiliar role of a leader of a platoon but in the unfamiliar role of the leader of a classroom, not dealing with the vicissitudes of battle but with the vicissitudes of parents, students, colleagues, and teaching. To be sure, the situations are different and the fatality rate among young teachers is not the same as the fatality rate among young second lieutenants; but their struggles to survive and learn have many of the same features.

Beginning teachers in classrooms, like new second lieutenants in battle, are special cases illustrating the consequences of two phenomena that are endemic to personnel systems. The first is that recruitment into any particular role in an organization will almost never yield the absolutely best person for that role. This is due partly to inefficiencies of matching individuals and jobs, inefficiencies that stem from such things as social norms, information limitations, the indivisibility of individuals' combinations of attributes and talents, and competency traps in learning from experience. However, it is also simply a necessary property of an assignment system. Efficient assignment allocates individuals to roles in terms of comparative, rather than absolute, advantage. The person who would be the best second lieutenant in the world may well serve the system better as a cartographer; and the person who would be the best teacher may serve the system better as an actor. No matter what the job is, it is always possible to identify individuals who would perform better than those who are assigned to the job by normal social processes, even efficient ones.

The second general organizational phenomenon is that training for a role inadequately captures the nature of the real thing. Performing as a physician is not well anticipated by training as a medical student. Leading a platoon in battle is not well anticipated by training as a cadet. Being a teacher is not well anticipated by teacher training. This is partly a criticism of the training, and training can often be improved to make it better anticipate life. However, the generality of the phenomenon suggests that it is not simply a problem with training but also stems from some fundamental difficulties both in communicating general knowledge and in integrating that knowledge with contextual knowledge.

It is tempting to attribute problems due to adverse recruitment and training to unique features of a particular job or organization. It is natural to look for ways to improve the recruitment and training of teachers or second lieutenants. Such a response is sensible, but it ignores the ubiquity of the problems. All jobs are filled by people who are not the best for the task, and all training will be less than perfect preparation for the real thing. That characteristic is not so much a failure of a personnel system as it is an unavoidable feature of it. The system can be made better, but the problems cannot be eliminated. They have to be coped with.

Cattani has intelligent ideas about improving the recruitment and training of new teachers, but she saves most of her energy for understanding how less than perfectly fit individuals can overcome their less than perfect training to achieve less than perfect but better performance. Unprepared and poorly equipped individuals can, nonetheless, learn to do a job. Energy and commitment can spawn competence, even style and grace. In its explorations of the magic and trauma of that process, this book is both a set of essays on becoming a teacher and a metaphor for life.

James G. March
Stanford University

Acknowledgments

Many people supported the research and writing of this book, and I wish to thank a few of them here. The six study teachers generously welcomed me into their classrooms and shared their teaching lives with me. Mike Atkin provided guidance and encouragement throughout the research process. Judith Haymore Sandholtz and Jerry Brodkey reviewed drafts and offered sound advice. Finally, Faye Zucker at Corwin Press was extraordinarily helpful and attentive in each stage of the book's production.

The following reviewers are also gratefully acknowledged:

Barbara Curry
Associate Professor
Department of Education
University of Delaware
Newark, DE

Jolinda Simes
Director
Career-In-Training Program
Minneapolis Public Schools
Minneapolis, MN

Marguerite Terrill
Associate Director
Teacher Education for Clinical and Field Experiences
Central Michigan University
Mount Pleasant, MI

Kim Truesdell
Associate Director
Teacher Education Institute
University at Buffalo
Buffalo, NY

About the Author

Dana Haight Cattani, a writer and researcher, holds a doctorate in curriculum and teacher education from Stanford University. She studies teacher education and induction, school/university collaboration, and the sociology of education. She has conducted qualitative evaluation of school reform and has been a university and school site supervisor of beginning teachers. A former elementary and high school English teacher, Dr. Cattani was a fellow and teacher consultant with the California Writing Project, where she published and presented classroom research. Currently, she is active in school governance and as a classroom volunteer in her local public schools. The mother of three, she lives with her family in Chapel Hill, North Carolina. Her e-mail address is dana_cattani@stanfordalumni.org.

1

Gender, Age, and Teacher Induction

While reviewing answers with the class on a multiple-choice homework assignment, the young teacher called on students from around the room, and they responded with correct answers that she readily accepted. However, the final response hung in the air, unaffirmed. The teacher scrutinized the answer key in front of her. After an awkward pause, she said, "I don't think that's the right answer." The students looked at each other quizzically, as if to say, "Doesn't she know?"

By her own account, this student teacher, whom I will call Vanessa, hesitated not because she was uncertain about the best response to the homework. Instead, her hesitation reflected uncertainty about how to convey to the student that there was a better answer than the one he had provided. She wanted to be encouraging and did not want to make the student lose face, especially in front of the class. Ironically, Vanessa's effort to protect the student resulted in a loss of face, nonetheless: her own. Her good intentions resulted in some self-inflicted damage to her authority.

In my past work as a university supervisor of teacher education students, I had the opportunity to visit a number of different schools and observe student teachers. The candidates—all young women—were engaging, intelligent, compassionate, and eager. However, I noticed some patterns in their performance that I came to believe were characteristic of many new teachers, and of young women in particular. These new teachers often seemed reluctant to inform students directly if an answer was incorrect, incomplete, or irrelevant. They were often uncomfortable in telling other people what to do, as teachers must. In general, they were loath to keep firm deadlines or impose penalties, even ones they had instituted in response to specific problems. They sometimes seemed averse to interacting with parents or administrators—even when appropriate and necessary—preferring to swallow their unmet needs, unfilled requests, or dissatisfactions rather than appear disgruntled or risk confrontation.

Given only this information, it might be tempting to conclude that Vanessa and her classmates were unsuitable candidates to become teachers. In my estimation, they were not. In fact, they were part of a pool of well-prepared teacher education students. Each had strong academic credentials and extensive past experience working with children and adolescents. In addition to these general qualifications, their teacher education included specific and appropriate course work in pedagogy. From all indications, these young women were ready to teach.

This book began as a response to Vanessa and the other university students I supervised. It evolved into an examination of six California teachers' professional lives. I highlight their paths toward instructional competence (mastery of curriculum, pedagogical skill, and classroom management), professional competence (facility with work relationships, career management, and the school bureaucracy), and cultural competence (awareness, sensitivity, and support of diverse populations). These teachers are all young white women working in the important and challenging setting of an urban school district, but many of the concerns they face are shared by male teachers, teachers of any ethnic background, and second-career or reentry teachers in any venue. The essential topics of race and class are part of these stories, although their analysis here is not comprehensive. Rather, the book is a portrait of teacher induction with particular attention to the synergy of gender and age in shaping expectations and outcomes. Its purpose is to promote greater instructional, professional, and cultural competence among all new teachers as well as improved teacher education and professional development.

YOUNG WOMEN TEACHERS

One might reasonably argue that young women teachers, particularly white young women teachers, do not need further study or attention. They are, after all, capable of earning a modest living in a union job with health benefits, lots of vacation, and stipends for extra assignments. Even if they find public school teaching discouraging and do not last long, these young women are likely to have sufficient skills and credentials to make their way in modern American society. Given the urgent and complex educational challenges of teacher shortages, assessment mandates, achievement gaps, and school violence, why focus on young women teachers?

The answer, briefly, is numbers. Women make up the vast majority of new teachers. Many of them are young. Most earn their bachelor's degrees and teaching credentials simultaneously (Feistritzer, 1990). While some of these new teachers might be older students, it is likely that many are fresh out of college, probably in their early twenties. The unexceptional new

> Gender Dynamics: Teacher Demographics
>
> - 73% of public school teachers are women (National Center for Education Statistics [NCES], 2000).
>
> - 74% of students in teacher education programs are women (Yasin, 1999).
>
> - 80% or more of elementary teachers are women (NCES, 1996).

teacher, in this book and in teacher education programs across the nation, is a young white woman from a middle-class background.

I focus on young women teachers because this group represents the primary assembly of new teachers, because this perspective is largely overlooked in past research, and because of the emergence of informative new findings in the area of women's psychological development and roles in organizations. These teachers' instructional competence influences student achievement. Their professional competence helps shape the quality of interactions within the school as well as between it and the surrounding community. New teachers' cultural competence determines, in part, the degree of inclusion and opportunity the school can offer all its students. Finally, current calls for school change emphasize the role of the teacher in collaborative school governance, community relations, curriculum development, and assessment (Anderson, Rolheiser, & Gordon, 1998; Black & Davern, 1998; Griffin, 1995; Heller & Firestone, 1995; Sizer, 1984; Smith, 1994). A more comprehensive understanding of the new teachers who might be expected to do this work—many of whom are young women—can make meaningful and productive change more feasible.

The Difficulty of Research on Gender

Attempting to understand gender differences is difficult, at best. When well done, it is illuminating without being prescriptive. Sound gender research highlights individual cases as well as wider trends, balancing idiosyncrasies and patterns. Nonetheless, thoughtful people disagree about how to talk about gender and what significance it has in schools. Some researchers prefer to minimize differences between men and women in an attempt to debunk stereotypes, while others champion these very differences as a way of legitimizing characteristics common to women. Still others may find any demarcation along gender lines contrived or needlessly divisive.

I believe that research on gender inevitably simplifies, even as it illuminates. I view people as both objects of socialization and autonomous agents, contributing to some general patterns with dramatic variation. This orientation allows for individuals to be idiosyncratic, capable of pettiness and intelligence, peevishness and courage. It does not reduce the complexity of the issues by lodging responsibility either in the school organization, where accountability is convoluted, or in the individual, where it can be easily and sometimes inappropriately pegged. Instead, I seek to preserve the autonomy and agency of the individuals while highlighting group phenomena, creating an empathic portrait of six different young women teachers.

Young White Women Teachers

Gender and age dynamics often generate complications for young women teachers. However, these complications pale beside the more dramatic and tumultuous issues that separate some students and parents from the predominantly white middle-class world of public schools (Biklen, 1993; Delpit, 1995; Lortie, 1975; Sikes, 1997). In terms of race (Delpit, 1995; Kozol, 1991; Paley, 1979; Wilson, 1987), ethnicity (Barber & Estrin, 1996; Bourgois, 1995; Rodriguez, 1982; Rose, 1989), and social class (Anyon, 1988; Bourdieu, 1986; Bowles & Gintis, 1975; Freire, 1970), this divide has been well charted. Its intersection with young white women teachers has not been.

Initially, I set out to study the effects of gender and age, two facets of social interaction where young women have subordinate status that can make their induction into teaching particularly difficult. I remain convinced that these issues profoundly influence new teachers' competence. However, as I became more deeply involved in observation and analysis of young women teachers at work in urban schools, it quickly became apparent that the complications of their professional lives could not be explained fully by focusing on their subordinate roles.

The teachers in this study are white, college-educated women who generally describe professional parents; stimulating school experiences; a youth in suburban neighborhoods; interests in art, music, and travel; and optimism about the future. While not exempt from family problems, financial concerns, and other setbacks, they share a sense of freedom from privation and of confidence in the power of education. Whether or not their youths qualify as strictly middle class, their present employment in schools certainly does (Lortie, 1975; Sikes, 1997).

Here lie the origins of a confounding twist for young white women teachers in urban settings. Although the teachers face significant concerns about the effects of gender and age in their professional lives, they customarily enjoy dominant status in terms of race, ethnicity, and class within their schools. This tangled combination of subordinate and dominant traits clouds ready understanding of the professional lives of young white wom-

---

Cultural Dynamics: Teacher Demographics

- 87% of elementary and secondary schoolteachers are white (Yasin, 1999).

- 80% of students in teacher education programs are white (Yasin, 1999).

- White women teachers tend to come from more affluent financial circumstances than their male peers or colleagues from other racial backgrounds (Dilworth, 1990; Lortie, 1975; Weiner, 1993).

---

en teachers, particularly in the urban school settings that are often unfamiliar to them.

At this time, it is important to try to attract a more diverse population of teachers in the United States. However, as a practical matter, it is also important to find ways to prepare and support the young women, most of whom are white, who will be teaching in our nation's diverse schools. This preparation and support hinges on commitment to the democratic goal of equal educational opportunity. Its hallmark is excellence in teaching, regardless of the composition of the school or its faculty.

THE MANTLE OF TEACHER

An important facet of preparing new teachers is a clear understanding of the importance of authority for teachers in general and the problems that it poses for young women. New teachers are sometimes surprised by the amount of authority they are granted in the classroom. To the extent that they control that setting, teachers can be very powerful people in the eyes of their students. Teachers assign grades; communicate with parents; and distribute the perquisites of the classroom, including desirable seats, special responsibilities, encouragement or affection, and academic or social subgroupings. They assign penalties ranging from reduced freedom at recess to retention in a grade for another year. They determine content and teaching methods: what gets taught and how.

However, that authority is sharply constrained by its circumstances. A teacher's judgments can evoke wrath. Grades, perquisites, and penalties must be assigned carefully or else the teacher risks confrontations with parents or administrators who may challenge her decisions. A teacher's options with regard to content and methods are constrained by available materials, expertise, and administrative support. In matters of discipline, resource allocation, and equity of assignments, new teachers often are left to fend for themselves, sometimes with disappointing results. Consequently, depending on the circumstances, the degree of authority for new teachers can be exhilarating or unsettling. Comfortable or not, authority is the mantle of a teacher and cannot be ignored or discounted without consequences.

Women and Authority

Though personality is not clearly fixed according to gender, some researchers contend that women are particularly likely to develop speech and behavior patterns that reflect a less familiar vision of authority (Cameron, 1994; Gilligan, 1982; Tannen, 1990). In some women, as with some men, these characteristics may reflect poor preparation and insecurity; in others, they may signify abiding confidence and comfort with diversity of thought. In either case, these more feminine characteristics may make negotiating a work environment difficult because they are contrary to the more direct, unambiguous style of interaction that is often associated with men and the institutions they historically have shaped and controlled.

One of those institutions is the school. Schools are somewhat unusual in that virtually all American children have a lengthy apprenticeship in them. Those who choose to go on and become teachers are often the kind of people who have led past lives of academic success and sufficient obedience to view school positively (Lindblad & Prieto, 1992; Schmidt & Knowles, 1995; Willower, 1969). Moreover, successful students with biases toward obedience are likely to be invested in the authority systems of schools—and perhaps even the larger society—either because those systems are themselves unquestioned institutions or because they are a means to a desired end. Compliance may be a natural or rational choice to these prospective teachers. In either case, the kinds of students who go on to become teachers are more likely to be experienced in submitting to authority than in exercising it.

Many of those students are young women. Their reasons for selecting the profession of teaching vary, but many cite the desire to nurture, help, encourage, and make a difference in the lives of children and youth (Biklen, 1995; Feistritzer, 1990; Weiner, 1993). Given this orientation, some new teachers find that determining what other people should do, evaluating performances, and assigning consequences can be discomfiting. In some cases, women have a difficult time viewing themselves as authorities, expressing themselves so that others will attend to their ideas, and tapping fully their professional training and abilities (Belenky, Clinchy, Goldberger, & Tarule, 1986). If it is true, as some researchers suggest, that women define themselves more in terms of relationships than power (Acker, 1995; Brown & Gilligan, 1992; Gilligan, 1982; Hollinger & Fleming, 1992; Magolda, 1995), then authority becomes a particularly vexing tool in the hands of young

Age Dynamics: Teacher Demographics

"In the next ten years, America will need to hire two million teachers to meet rising enrollment demand and replace an aging teaching force. Half of our nation's teachers will retire during this time period" (Recruiting New Teachers, 2001).

women teachers. If they do not develop and use a traditional authoritative stance, they are unlikely to be recognized as proper teachers and granted whatever legitimacy and respect accompany that role. However, if they do develop and use such a stance, they may feel co-opted into a hierarchical relation that undermines the very values and ideals that drew them to teaching.

New Teachers, New Adults

The problem of authority is compounded for young women teachers by their age. These new teachers are not insecure adolescents, but neither are they fully formed adult professionals. They are something in between, and the transitional state of their lives is an important part of their experience as teachers. The transformation from student to professional employee is a difficult one for many new teachers as they learn to negotiate uncharted situations. Change is generally stressful, and if a change also includes assuming for the first time the responsibilities of working in an adult role, managing a career, and learning the technical skills required for a new job, the stress is compounded. New teachers may find themselves isolated in their classrooms or forging professional networks that are more important than the teachers can yet fathom. After years of grades and rankings as students, they may find the cursory employee evaluations of teachers to be neglectful and demeaning or may interpret the absence of praise as a reproach. They may be taken aback by the unexpected hostility from students that often accompanies compulsory attendance in schools and by the discovery that they are the arbiters of punishments and rewards when what they wanted was to be liked (Dreeben, 1973; Peshkin, 1988).

Further, young teachers may find that their age is both an asset and a liability. Youth is advantageous in a profession that requires a tremendous amount of energy. Young teachers may be perceived as ebullient and full of fresh ideas, ideal candidates for working with children. On a cultural level, American society idolizes youthful looks. This premium on youth is pronounced for women, who sometimes attract attention based more on appearances than accomplishments. Young women teachers, arguably in the prime of their physical lives, ought to be in an enviable position. However, youth is not always optimal. It often signals—rightly—inexperience, naïveté, and even ignorance. In this sense, youth is less desirable and certainly less powerful than maturity, with its greater wisdom and perspective. Young women teachers, who may encounter difficulties with authority because of their gender, then face the added burden of low status as youthful newcomers in the profession. The effect of this compounded load can be frustration, burnout, and turnover.

Young adults also tend to live in physical transition, having few ties that bind them to one location or job. This mobility contributes to one of every six new teachers changing jobs within the first year (Dornbusch, Glasgow, & Lin, 1996). As well, since teachers can enter the field after relatively modest educational or financial investment and can take a hiatus without great fear of technological change or skill obsolescence, many feel free to try teaching briefly as an experiment. Neither sex demonstrates particular commitment to classroom teaching, with men often leaving for administration or other professions and women often leaving—sometimes temporarily—for child rearing and family obligations (Dreeben, 1973; Peshkin, 1992). The professional lives of young women are often more circuitous than those of their male counterparts, and this phenomenon may contribute to a perception that these women lack dedication to work (Hollinger & Fleming, 1992). The fact that most new teachers are young adults has significant bearing on their career patterns.

Furthermore, age and particularly gender often determine a teacher's social networks with colleagues, which, in turn, determine her access to power, resources, and influence as well as her vulnerability to outside control (McPherson & Smith-Lovin, 1986, 1987). Since people often congregate socially according to gender, age, and interests, it is likely that young women will be spending any discretionary work time with other young teachers, especially other young women, none of whom may be tapped into the streams of power. They become, in effect, segregated within schools, not by design but through the norms of social interaction. Regardless, the resulting isolation limits their authority in the broader school context.

THE STUDY

In the days prior to the start of each school year, new teachers enter silent and lifeless classrooms where they dust and arrange and organize. However, the quickening of an inert classroom into a vibrant and vital center of learning cannot occur until the teacher has developed a degree of instructional, professional, and cultural competence. The speed and the scale of that teacher's growth directly influence the outer bounds of student achievement in that room. For the sake of those students and of their teachers, articulating steps toward competence can help expedite this critical process.

In order to explore the ways that new teachers develop this competence, I worked with six elementary teachers in a large urban school district in the San Francisco Bay Area. The teachers' ages ranged from 24 to 30. All were white women. They had between one and four years' previous teaching experience. During a five-month period in the late 1990s, I observed their classes, attended parent functions, ate lunch in the teachers' lounges, trailed them to the office, attended staff development meetings, and interviewed them about their work. I have given them the pseudonyms Stephanie, Helen, Paula, Beth, Karen, and Julie. These teachers worked in a school district that served a largely African American and Latino population, with significant groups of Asians and Pacific Islanders as well. White students were a minority in the district. Except for Julie, the study teachers worked at schools in relatively impoverished areas.

Each of the following six chapters profiles an individual teacher along with supporting or contrasting examples from other teachers. Chapter 2 introduces Stephanie and the paradox of authority for young women teachers. Chapter 3 features Helen and the notion of professional identity. Paula is the main character in Chapter 4, an analysis of school culture and its bearing on new teachers. Administration is the focus of Chapter 5, with Beth as its primary subject teacher. Chapter 6 examines the notion of professional judgment, relying primarily on experiences from Karen's teaching. Chapter 7 describes Julie's school environment, which was characterized—at least ostensibly—by affirmation and attainment. Chapter 8 considers the significance of race, ethnicity, and social class in the experiences of young white women teachers. Finally, Chapter 9 concludes with practical applications of these ideas for new teachers and those who work with them.

2

Stephanie
The Paradox of Authority

> There has long been reluctance on the part of teachers and
> those who have studied them to think of teaching in terms of
> relationships involving power and authority.
>
> *R. Dreeben*

A second-year teacher in an urban school, Stephanie is an accomplished musician, a critical reader, and the bearer of a master's degree in education from a prestigious university. She is bright, lively, and affable, well qualified by training and disposition to be an elementary school teacher. However, her credibility and effectiveness are constrained, in part, by one of the more vexing paradoxes a young woman teacher faces. As a teacher, she is a person of authority. However, as a young woman, she may have little authority, particularly in professional matters. She may have imagined that the credential or the title or even the chalk carried with it the requisite authority to do the job. It does not.

AUTHORITY WITH COLLEAGUES

A new teacher, particularly a young woman, is a kind of upstart. Suddenly, with the conferral of a credential, she is graduated from student to teacher, presumably with all of the rights and responsibilities of that role. However, like an enlisted recruit who is promoted to officer, she may not have the social standing to be accepted fully by her new peers. They may welcome her, they may offer support, but they are unlikely to treat her as a peer, since, in truth, she is not one. She lacks the familiarity with the setting, the professional knowledge, and the comparable life experience that characterize established peers. Over time, she may acquire these shared traits and

> Meet the Teacher: Stephanie
>
> Age: 24
>
> Education: B.A. Music, M.A. Education
>
> Professional Training: Teaching credential
>
> Number of Years Teaching: 2
>
> Grade Level: 4th
>
> Class Size: 32
>
> School Enrollment: 400
>
> Schoolwide Eligibility for Subsidized Lunch: 50%
>
> Schoolwide Student Ethnicity: 50% African American, 25% Asian, 25% Other
>
> Schoolwide Achievement Scores Compared With National Average: Significantly below

more. In the meantime, however, forming authoritative connections with coworkers can be problematic.

Supervisor Relationships

In hierarchical relationships, the relative position of each person is clear. Every subordinate reports to a boss, who in turn has a different boss. In the loose accountability of schools, teachers generally report to administrators, with new teachers doing most of the reporting. However, teachers are the immediate supervisors of instructional aides and other classroom support personnel.

Instructional Aides

Clearly, there is a supervisory relationship between a teacher and any instructional aides who work in her classroom. These aides are individuals hired to assist the classroom teacher and increase the ratio of adults to students. Aides are not credentialed teachers, and they have no direct responsibilities for curriculum, pedagogy, or assessment. They are hourly employees who report to the classroom teacher, and she, in turn, evaluates their work. They do not evaluate her work.

Stephanie worked with two African American instructional aides, Josephine and Alonzo. (All names have been changed.) Josephine was scheduled to work from 8:30 a.m. to 11:30 a.m. every day, although she routinely arrived for work fifteen to thirty minutes late. According to Stephanie, Josephine took responsibility for driving several nieces and nephews to school, and her promptness depended on their readiness. This chronic lagging did not seem to bother Stephanie. She explained, "Well, if she's not here on time, it's okay. I have gotten over it. I just don't expect her to be here at 8:30. She usually gets here at 8:45."

As offenses go, tardiness is not particularly heinous, but in the context of a three-hour workday and a clock-driven school culture, it is significant. Interestingly, Stephanie puts the onus on herself to "[get] over it." Apparently, she has abandoned any expectation that Josephine arrive promptly as opposed to encouraging Josephine to figure out a way to get to work on time. By compensating for the deficiency herself, Stephanie sidesteps the need for confrontation. The problem is resolved. She internalizes it as a way of avoiding possible confrontation. Stephanie's behavior seemed indicative of her genuine affection for Josephine and of their warm friendship. Nevertheless, this degree of accommodation set a precedent that undermined Stephanie's authority.

Stephanie's interactions with Alonzo were not as cordial. Alonzo assisted students with learning disabilities by attending class with them and helping them focus on the lesson. He was a long-term substitute, not a permanent staff member. He was younger than Stephanie, but although their ages were close, the sharp differences in their education, job status, race, and life experiences permeated their dealings. Stephanie admitted, "We haven't had a lot of positive interactions."

In contrast to her warm, personal connection to Josephine, Stephanie chafed at any blurring of the status distinctions that separated her from Alonzo. For example, she recounted an incident when a janitor asked her age. When she told him she was 24 years old, he said, "You don't look a day over 21." Stephanie replied, "Well, I am. You have to be at least 22 to be a teacher because you have to be a college graduate." The janitor replied, "Well, Alonzo is a teacher, and he's only 21."

Stephanie was irked. Whether the janitor simply inferred or Alonzo actually claimed that he was a teacher, in Stephanie's mind, Alonzo misrepresented himself. In fact, *teacher* is both a description and an official role. Alonzo does teach students, but his formal role is instructional aide, not certificated teacher. In the janitor's mind, that distinction may not be significant, but in Stephanie's view, it certainly is. She clearly resents the three years the janitor has unwittingly shaved from her majority. To the degree that her authority rests on her age and experience, those three years are crucial. They help separate her from Alonzo, as well as from the janitor. She is miffed when others are casual about their reckoning of this authority, perhaps especially when it is not in her favor.

Stephanie's interactions with these two aides reveal ambivalence about her role as a supervisor. Neither aide is a model employee. In fact, Alonzo

Worth Discussing: Supervising Adults

- An instructional aide who has been working at the school for many years is assigned to your classroom. Repeatedly, the aide corrects you or gives students instructions contrary to yours. How might you respond to this aide's behavior?

- Another instructional aide wants you to direct her every move and then approve it when completed. You are busy with other students and irritated by the interruptions. How might you respond to this aide's behavior?

was fired the next year after making suggestive remarks to some girls and swearing at some boys. Josephine, on the other hand, took some special reading training over the summer and returned to school with enhanced skills. Josephine ostensibly makes supervision easy, while Alonzo pushes Stephanie to rein him in. When she does, it is with a vengeance. She is vindictive and resentful of the need to be supervisory.

New teachers find themselves in an awkward position as they supervise other adults in the school (England, 1992). Often unaccustomed to mixing peer interactions with evaluative responsibilities, new teachers may find themselves hard pressed to provide appropriate feedback, especially to colleagues who are older or have more seniority at the school. If the colleague is a friend, providing critical feedback may jeopardize the relationship, or so it might appear to a new teacher whose sense of professional obligation may be tempered by affection. If the colleague is not a friend, a new teacher may be no less reluctant to provide feedback, either in hopes of avoiding confrontation or because she deems the relationship not worth the trouble. In either case, the effect is reticence. Leaving unsaid things that ought to be said is not authoritative. It is timid, if not irresponsible and unprofessional. This problem is not limited to new teachers; it is characteristic of many employees in schools and other places. However, for young women, its effects are magnified by an existing authority deficit. As a college-educated, tenure-track teacher, Stephanie has more official status than either of the two aides with whom she works. In one case, she tries to render this status difference invisible, and in the other, she underscores it heavily. She compromises her authority, first by ignoring and then by insisting on it.

Colleague Relationships

While there is a distinct pecking order in the relationships between faculty and instructional aides, that dynamic is much more muted within the faculty itself. Officially, there is little hierarchy among teachers. They share

> ### Gender Dynamics: Perceptions of Power
>
> Power is one facet of authority, perhaps the part that is most uncharacteristic of young women teachers. The notion of power itself may seem unbecoming, in part because it is frequently associated with inappropriate greed or ambition, with dominion over others, or with ruthlessness (Acker, 1995). However, in a more positive sense, power can be construed as the ability to get things done, to make credible promises of rewards or consequences. This kind of power is rooted in competence, and its fruit is credibility. Wise new teachers cultivate access to and facility with such power.

the same job title and near-flat career ladder. Nominally, their status is comparable, but gender and age do create aggravating complications for young women teachers. Consequently, there is an informal ranking among teachers, and new young women tend to be relegated to the bottom.

Other Young Women Teachers

Ostensibly, in interactions among new teachers, there is no hierarchy. This peer connection presents different problems with authority. For instance, Stephanie and two other new young women teachers were assigned to participate as a team in a two-year science leadership institute. As part of their work, they organized a faculty inservice session where teachers would meet in grade cluster groups to create a science curriculum rubric. Stephanie hoped that this rubric would document which science topics and kits teachers used in each grade with the goal of forging a more organized and systematic science curriculum for the students.

However, construction of the rubric turned out to be little more than each teacher justifying her proprietary right to teach her favorite units, defending her friends' preferences, and shunting off unfavored kits to absentee parties, preferably at other schools. There was little mention of pedagogical reasons for introducing certain topics at certain ages or in certain sequences. It was a practical and efficient way of completing the task at hand, but the opportunity for meaningful discussion of curriculum went unfulfilled.

In fairness to Stephanie, she had little help. As a result of illness, an appointment, and a district commitment, neither of the other two teachers on her team attended the planning session or the inservice meeting. They made no arrangements to share in the preparation or presentation. Stephanie was clearly annoyed but said, "I don't feel like arguing . . . right now." Ultimately, there was little preparation even by Stephanie, perhaps in part because she was disheartened by her colleagues' disregard for the project.

Worth Discussing: Monitoring Colleagues

You notice that the teacher next door is sometimes late for class. The students wait outside the classroom after the bell has rung. This same person seems to show videos at least once or twice a week. Should you do anything? If so, what? What are the possible ramifications?

It's not clear when—if ever—Stephanie does feel like arguing. Reluctant to express opinions to her colleagues, she admitted, "I never say anything in faculty meetings just because I don't want to rock the boat. I don't know, I like to stay out of things, out of the whole political thing." Not wanting to "rock the boat" may make for fewer conflicts, but others may interpret this stance as weak. It also may mean countenancing substandard performance—in this case, her peers' neglect of their obligation. It may also lead to low expectations. Two days after the inservice meeting, Stephanie felt that it had been a success—not on account of the quality of the rubrics, which she had not seen—but because none of her colleagues had left negative notes in her box. While the absence of complaints can be its own kind of success, especially for a new leader, it is not resounding evidence of progress.

Why do new teachers not hold each other more accountable? Presumably, they refrain from intervening for many of the same reasons that most peers do not hold each other accountable. They may assume that monitoring others' behavior is not their place. It may be that teachers, particularly new teachers, grapple with so many conflicts in their dealings with students that their reserves of energy for colleague relationships are depleted. As well, colleague relationships are the more permanent and therefore require extra caution. In addition, teachers work in isolation and often cannot verify any concerns about each other, so it is easiest to ignore them. Finally, teachers may assume, perhaps correctly, that they will reap the clemency they sow. It makes sense to tread lightly on colleague relationships, especially for new teachers who may be eager to make friends at work. As a result, there is great reluctance to report lapses or even to ask colleagues to do anything that might be inconvenient.

Veteran Teacher Colleagues

Although Stephanie and the veteran teachers at her school are colleagues, they are not true peers. Their behavior reveals subtle but significant status differences. For example, during the science inservice that Stephanie led, her colleagues were pleasant but ultimately disrespectful and impolite. The faculty divided into two groups, and Stephanie's group met in one of the classrooms. While Stephanie gathered information for the continuum, her colleagues worked on a variety of unrelated projects in an inadvertent display of disregard. The woman who taught in that room wandered around attending to paperwork and other projects. One teacher abruptly left half an hour early. Another teacher stepped out during the discussion and shortly returned with an art project that she was working on in preparation for an upcoming field trip.

It seems unlikely that Stephanie would have behaved this way during an inservice led by one of these colleagues. Of course, teachers are busy, and afternoons quickly become evenings. Most schools have the quiet teachers who sit in the back of faculty meetings, grading papers and listening with one ear, if at all. It is the blatancy of the inattention that is surprising. The teachers made little, if any, attempt to hide their divided attention. They all seem to like Stephanie. They are nice to her. But they do not treat her with professional courtesy. As is common in elementary schools, all of them are women. Perhaps someone of greater stature than Stephanie, or someone who conveyed greater urgency, or someone who had prepared more thoroughly or raised a more compelling issue, might have garnered greater attentiveness. Stephanie shares some responsibility for the diffuse focus. However, in a culture of meager accountability in general, new teachers have little chance of leading boldly.

Youth is a factor. Stephanie's colleagues are typically a generation older than she is. She explained, "Their children are older than me. A lot of people I work with, like, their children are 28, 29, married." This difference is neither invisible nor irrelevant. It influences the way Stephanie's colleagues treat her, for better and worse. Stephanie reported, "I definitely feel like there is a mentality of people trying to take care of me and watch out for me, which is really nice."

Formally, the connection of veteran colleagues to new teachers is not hierarchical. Yet in fact, there is a status hierarchy at play. As young people, they have a lieutenant relationship with their colleagues, which, as Stephanie freely admits, has its advantages. However, it has disadvantages as well, particularly with regard to authority. It means that new teachers have junior status, which implies a need to defer, agree, or at least keep quiet. It is an art form that Stephanie performs well.

Mixed Signals

Achieving a degree of authority with colleagues is a tricky business. Faculties can be close communities with established social networks organized according to age, sex, grade level, subject area, or avocation. A sponsoring mentor, either formal or informal, provides a new teacher with one logical means of entrance. Under the best circumstances, this kind of relationship is productive and mutually rewarding. By definition, however, a new teacher and her mentor are not true peers. For the new teacher, this role can become restrictive and even patronizing, particularly if it does not

> ### Age Dynamics: The Ongoing Apprenticeship
>
> Youth and inexperience can profoundly shape the status of new teachers. Often, seasoned teachers' words carry more weight, their votes are more influential, and their private conversations with the principal make a greater difference than any similar efforts their junior colleagues might make. These veterans have been around long enough to see fads come and go, leaders change, students grow up and leave the schoolyard and return. Such teachers have insight and wisdom that new people cannot match. However, new teachers, who may have thought that their apprenticeship ended with student teaching, may be disheartened to discover that their competence is constrained not only by inexperience but also by their limited status and power within the school organization.

assume a more egalitarian flavor over time. Ironically, the presence of a mentor, particularly one who is performing her mentor functions conscientiously, may erode a new teacher's authority. This problem may be amplified for women, who tend to place great value on attachment and may be less willing to risk offense by changing the tone of the relationship or cultivating other allies (Gilligan, 1982). Or young women teachers may like being shielded and may come to rely on it, further damaging their own authority.

Alternately, a new teacher might be ignored, inadvertently excluded from much collegial interaction simply because her colleagues know from experience that few of these new recruits last long or because the teacher herself feels removed by age from most of her colleagues. Isolation undermines a new teacher's authority by cutting her off from the informal social networks that can enhance credibility. Disconnection makes her less aware of others' similar situations and less confident of her own actions. Many new teachers want to be independent enough to be credible in their own right but connected enough to be part of a community. Striking this authoritative balance with colleagues is no easy task, particularly for young women. Whether their colleagues' impulses are to protect them, ignore them, or help them, the fact remains: They are not peers.

AUTHORITY WITH PARENTS

The difficulties with authority do not end with colleagues. Parents also can pose complex challenges to young women teachers. At times, there seem to be conflicting and sometimes inappropriate expectations about the role of

> ### Age Dynamics: Parenting Skills
>
> "People [think that] you are a teacher so you have all these parenting skills, but I don't. And then other people treat me [as if] I am a child and I don't have any parenting skills and [as if] I shouldn't be in charge of their child."
>
> Stephanie

teacher. The confusion often centers on the relevance of formal training and life experience. Parents give varying degrees of credence to a teacher's academic background and professional education. Since her formal education tends to be public and indisputable, it is often to a young woman teacher's advantage when parents consider it important. Parents also weigh variably a teacher's other life experience: her age, marital status, experience as a parent, and degree of familiarity with aspects of the culture the parents value most. Depending on the circumstances, a teacher may find herself in an awkward situation where her specific formal training and life experience are given either too much or too little emphasis.

For young women, this problem can be particularly pronounced. With the shaky authority of a young woman and the generally indistinguishable education of teachers, her life experience takes on express significance. Some parents take comfort in the notion that their child's teacher is also a parent, and that fact may undermine the credibility of teachers who do not have children of their own, regardless of their sex. However, because American society traditionally assigns women the task of child rearing, young women teachers face greater expectations to be knowledgeable about parenting, whether or not they are parents (Sikes, 1997). For any of these reasons, young women teachers may find establishing authoritative relationships with parents to be complicated.

The Trouble With Parents

Certainly, positive working relationships with parents are helpful to authoritative teaching. However, the ubiquitous assumption of teaching that parent involvement is good may not always hold true for inexperienced teachers. The trouble with parents is also their quintessential virtue: They want what is best for their child. Unfortunately, what they want may not be reasonable, fair, or appropriate from the teacher's perspective. Her commission is to attend to the needs of the collective class, given the resources and skills at her disposal. In this situation, conflict is likely. When the teacher is a young woman, the dynamics may be particularly strained. Parents may be emboldened to assert forcefully their wishes or opinions or

Tips for New Teachers: Working With Parents

- Listen attentively to parents.

- Validate their concerns, and consider their suggestions. Their knowledge of their child gives them privileged insights.

- Suggest specific ways that they can help their child, and describe upcoming units of study or assignments so that the parents will know what to anticipate.

- Do not commit to actions that you cannot or should not take.

- Do not apologize for things that are not your fault.

- Be clear in your own mind about what is negotiable and what is not.

demands, knowing that the teacher may defer to their judgment or will at least listen politely. The young women teachers themselves, who perhaps are getting more—and more intense—feedback than their colleagues, often feel obliged to try to accommodate the varying demands. As a result, some young women teachers in particular find that frequent parent encounters increase their anxiety, distract their focus, and inflate the number of people they feel bound to try to please. Ironically, although parent involvement is one indicator of support and reinforcement at home, some young women teachers find that parents are best seen at Parent Night and not heard from again.

However, as with the role of the teacher, there are also conflicting and sometimes inappropriate notions of the role of the parent. Teachers who are not parents themselves may be prone to simplifying the complex undertaking of raising a child, assuming that a few simple, correct choices lead to felicitous results. Or these teachers may find bothersome the parents who ask questions instead of simply trusting the institution of the school to act in the best interests of their child. It may be tempting to believe that the parents' job is to support them, forgetting that the parents' goals for the child may not mirror their own. Teachers who are parents themselves may understand more intuitively parents' concerns. Of course, the parents want the child to grow and develop, but they usually have ideas about what kind of adult they want that child to become, as well (Ruddick, 1980). It is unwise and undesirable for the teacher to become inured to discounting parents.

In any case, relationships with parents are formidable and cause for much concern among new teachers. Finding an authoritative stance is difficult, particularly given the many different kinds of parents with whom teachers interact. While there are a host of possible descriptions, parents who are distraught, impassive, or confrontational pose special difficulties

Age Dynamics: Advising Parents

"I had a parent last year who was my age, and she had a nine-year-old son. And she used to come in crying because her son walked all over her and she was, like, *What will I do, what will I do?* And I was just, like, *I don't know what to do.* And she had had him when she was 14, and I was just, like, *I am 24 years old, I don't know how to help you.* And she has two children and she is my age, and I can hardly take care of my dog."

Stephanie

for inexperienced teachers. Not surprisingly, parents who are supportive evoke profound gratitude and respect.

Distraught Parents

Distraught parents are overwhelmed by the demands of their children and look to the teacher as a source of guidance. While this arrangement has some advantages for the teacher—specifically, the fact that she has the parents' attention—it can be awkward and uncomfortable for her. Distraught parents often seek advice, assuming or perhaps simply hoping that the teacher knows something they do not about motivating or disciplining or helping their child. Often implied in their behavior is not confidence in the teacher's training or experience so much as desperation.

Stephanie readily acknowledged that she did not always know how to advise parents, but she was clear about their responsibilities. Of child rearing, she said, "That is [the parents'] job. Maybe they need to figure out a way to become more educated about how to raise a child." However, the job of being a parent is fundamentally unlike the job of being a classroom teacher. In fact, being a parent is not technically a job at all, in the sense of a routine activity for which one is paid. It has no prerequisites, no certification, no formal training, no evaluation. Like teachers, parents learn while on duty, often through their mistakes. Stephanie's notion of the role of parent seems to draw more heavily on the model of teacher education than on the reality of being a parent. In any case, she comes across as naïve, which is not authoritative.

Impassive Parents

Other parents seem more impassive. They do not seek the teacher's counsel nor do they challenge her. At times inscrutable and aggravating, they offer little help or support. Their general reticence may imply embarrassment or anger or intimidation or confusion or trust or preoccupation or

> ### Cultural Dynamics: Understanding Parents' Actions
>
> "Often, middle-class school professionals are appalled by what they see of poor parents, and most do not have the training or the ability to see past surface behaviors to the meanings behind parents' actions," according to educator Lisa Delpit (1995, p. 175). Effective teachers resist making snap judgments about parents' motives or values. Instead, these teachers seek information and understanding as they work with parents of all backgrounds to promote student achievement.

resentment, any part of which may be directed at the teacher and rooted in their perception of her.

Stephanie was clearly frustrated by her dependence on parents who were unable or unwilling to assist her in influencing their children. For instance, she described a parent conference attended by a student, his father, and a translator.

> This boy, Vincent, just screws around all the time. And he is really smart. . . . And I was telling Vincent's dad this and he actually speaks Chinese and so a translator was talking and he was just, like, *Oh yeah, Vincent is just like that at home, too. I don't know what to do with him.* And I just said, Well, it has got to stop. . . . It is not okay for Vincent to be like that at home or at school. He can't run the household, and he can't run the school. And so [the translator] tells Vincent's father that and he was, like, *Well, I know.* And I ask him, What is going to change? How are you going to change his behavior? And he was, like, *I don't know.* And I was just angry. And I just thought, Why did I drag [you] in here to talk to [Vincent] if you are not going to even help?

Clearly, this encounter made Stephanie feel thwarted. It seems reasonable to assume that it was dissatisfying—at least—to Vincent and his father, as well. Certainly, the cultural and linguistic differences are sharp limitations, and the father is at a disadvantage in this conversation. Shame, misunderstanding, or disagreement may color his response. Perhaps the father is irritated to be called to the school, embarrassed by the son's behavior, concerned about his son's performance, shamed by the young woman whose frustration must have been evident. Vincent sees his father look passive and unprepared, like a student unable to answer a teacher's pointed question in class. Presumably, Stephanie called this conference in an effort to increase pressure on Vincent to cooperate, having exhausted other, easier means of persuasion. She needs this conference to go well in order to reinforce the soundness and rationality of her expectations for him. To her chagrin, she discovers that she has the power to belittle this father but not to procure his support.

A more authoritative teacher might need to rely less on parental endorsement or enforcement. There is authority implicit in her calling this conference, but she wields it in a heavy-handed and not particularly skillful manner when she turns it on the father. It is a demonstration to be expected from one who has little authority and is unaccustomed to using it. In this situation, some parents would at least offer the lip service of a verbal commitment in order to save face and expedite the end of the conference. For whatever reason, this father did not, or if he did, it was such cold comfort that Stephanie failed to include it in her retelling of the story. He may have wanted more time to think or to discuss the matter with Vincent. He may not have known what to say. In any case, his relative silence leaves Stephanie looking ineffective and blustery, unable to motivate the father *or* the son.

Confrontational Parents

While Stephanie is frustrated by the distraught parents and irritated by the impassive ones, her greatest ire is reserved for the confrontational parents. These parents often assume that they know more than the teacher. They expect that their significant investment as parents, as well as their life experience in a variety of other roles, gives them the prerogative to shape their child's formal schooling. If the teacher is obviously young and inexperienced, confrontational parents may be particularly suspicious of her ability to meet their expectations. They may be right. If she is female, they may feel free to assert their opinions and demands baldly, believing that she will capitulate rather than argue.

Stephanie seems to believe that the role of parents is to validate her authority by bringing to bear their own influence to reinforce her efforts. She described an encounter with the mother of one of her students in this way:

> This woman, she thinks she really has got her act together and she works at Kaiser [Permanente, a large health maintenance organization]. . . . She has raised three daughters by herself and she had done a good job and she is a very put-together looking woman. . . . But I guess she is just convinced she has better ideas about how her daughters should be educated. And she can't really give me any examples, but she is just always questioning what I am doing.

Finding this behavior provoking, Stephanie explained, "Then I get all theoretical and highfalutin." She told the mother, "Well, if you want to know why I am doing this, it is because of this study and this study and this study." In effect, Stephanie holds up the shield of research to protect her from parents who question her practices. Invoking studies the mother is

> ### Cultural Dynamics: Whose Research and for What Purpose?
>
> "People of color are, in general, skeptical of research as a determiner of our fates. Academic research has, after all, found us genetically inferior, culturally deprived, and verbally deficient" (Delpit, 1995, p. 31).

unlikely to be familiar with is a calculated conversation-stopper. They cannot be refuted, not because they are incontestable but because they are unknown. When Stephanie believes that her authority is in question, she conjures as her defense vague and mysterious research, which is often distorted when distilled into a sentence or phrase. Recognizing her actions as a ploy, she explained, "I am credentialed to teach [her] child and that should be enough as far as I am concerned. I mean, there are lots of people that are teaching children that aren't credentialed to teach. I don't know why this parent gives me such a hard time." Stephanie puts more faith in the credential than might be warranted, but her point is clear: She does not appreciate having her authority challenged.

It is understandable for new teachers like Stephanie to want their formal preparation to be viewed as incontrovertible evidence that their judgments and authority are above reproach. Likewise, it is perfectly understandable for many parents to place more emphasis on life experience, particularly experience with children like theirs, than on training they may view as cursory or faddish. As they know, and as certificated teachers may be loath to admit, degrees and credentials do not a teacher make. They may be necessary, but that fact does not make them sufficient.

Supportive Parents

Happily, there are success stories. Stephanie described a more satisfying conference with Lamont's mother, who worked as an instructional aide at another school in the district. Stephanie said, "I never knew anyone could talk as much as Lamont," and when she sent him out of class, "he got real whiny and disrespectful." During the ensuing conference with his mother, Stephanie reported, "We talked for a while and it was really great. She was, like, *I know my son, I know he does this, and we're going to be on top of it.*" In validating Stephanie's version of events, "she was just really, really supportive and said she would stick by me 100% and follow through at home." For Stephanie, "it was just really positive because she really understood and appreciated being called." In Stephanie's judgment, Lamont's mother "knows what's going on."

What's going on may be that this mother believes that, regardless of the details, it is best for the child if the parent and teacher present a united front.

Tips for New Teachers: Successful Parent Phone Calls

- Keep phone calls focused and brief.

- Identify yourself and say immediately, "This is not an emergency. I'm calling because . . ."

- When appropriate, frame problems in terms of academic performance. Make the connections explicit ("Yolanda's tardiness and her talking during class are preventing her from doing her best work").

- If the interaction becomes charged or hostile, calmly reiterate your purpose for calling and bring the conversation to a close.

Whether or not it is better for the child, it certainly is easier for the teacher, especially a new teacher. Children may transfer their understanding of authoritative adults from parents to teachers. The incongruence between home and school is diminished, making the teacher's job easier.

Limited Partners

New teachers must figure out a way to communicate with all kinds of parents. For Stephanie, this responsibility means a balancing act. At the same time that she is critical of some parents, she is mindful of her own inexperience. Stephanie acknowledged, "I think I am not firm enough with parents a lot of times. I worry about coming across—you know, I am just a young person and I don't have children." Although she interrupts herself, presumably she worries about coming across as a pretender, someone who doles out advice that she has never tried herself. Stephanie's critique of herself is illustrative of the poorly defined relationship teachers and parents have. Stephanie hints at the tangle of concerns that characterize the relationships between teachers and parents.

Ideally, parents and teachers pool their shared interest and expertise, but in reality, their relationship is often an involuntary and sometimes unpalatable limited partnership. Each side may feel bound by decisions the other controls. If parents and teachers are to function as a team, then they should have some common understanding of the purposes of school and the desired means of achieving them. Few parents and teachers interact often enough to develop this kind of common vision, particularly since the impetus for many of their conversations is bad news. As well, the many cultures that come together in public schools guarantee salient differences among the key players. The common goals and practices that generally characterize partnerships are conspicuously absent in the relationship between parents and teachers.

New teachers face difficulties as they attempt to develop an authoritative stance with parents. The variables among parents are immense: different cultural backgrounds, linguistic backgrounds, educational expectations, social classes, and temperaments, at least. An authoritative teacher learns how to cultivate productive relationships with parents and take advantage of the benefits they can bring. The truly daunting fact about time-consuming and sometimes stressful relationships with parents is that they are a background concern. Ultimately, parents are peripheral to the most urgent challenge new teachers face: developing authority with their students.

AUTHORITY WITH STUDENTS

Authority with students comes, in part, from the institutional role of teacher. Students know that the teacher has the obligation and presumably the competence to teach them. They also know that, at least nominally, her role includes the enforcement of behavioral and academic standards. Institutional authority alone does not capture the essence of student-teacher interactions. Personal authority, or its absence, is vital to understanding classroom dynamics. This authority comes from students' great familiarity with the person who is their teacher. They sniff out her insecurities, her biases, her passions, her level of affection for them. Part of their willingness to respect her authority grows directly out of that knowledge. There is an intimacy in spending the school year together that can breed contempt or regard, depending on the situation. The most obvious manifestation of the teacher's authority is often classroom management.

Classroom Management

Schools are based on an unwritten pact between students and teachers. Teachers agree to prepare and present lessons, and students agree to listen and participate. Compulsory education undermines this tacit understanding and creates a need for teachers to respond to students who do not wish to be in class. Classroom management is terribly mundane, so mundane that new teachers sometimes fail to recognize how terribly revealing it is of their pedagogical skill. There is artistry even in keeping the peace. Classroom management is a keystone on which most other authority must rest. A teacher who has poor control in the classroom is unlikely to be credible to colleagues or administrators, to parents or students. Even wonderful lessons can be undermined by the tenor of a classroom. Teachers who fail to understand this rudimentary truth are unlikely to achieve a satisfactory degree of authority until they can address this prerequisite of instruction. New teachers, including young women, are particularly at risk of having inadequate classroom management on account of their own low status, their general reluctance to confront problems, and their desire to be liked by their students.

More so than with adults, Stephanie was remarkably direct and forthright in her conversations with students. She seemed resolute and in command as she handled the obvious, flagrant violations of classroom life. When a boy shouted, "Shut up!" at another boy in the class, Stephanie was mobilized. "*You* are gonna leave!" she ordered. She wrote a pass, and the student was gone. Her action was decisive and unambiguous. She had an intuitive understanding of the line dividing acceptable conduct from unacceptable, and she was not reluctant to impose sanctions as necessary. She did not seem to question her role in this matter, instead trusting her instincts. On another occasion, when an arithmetic homework assignment was due, Stephanie asked a boy, "Where's your math?" He replied, "I didn't do it. It was too complicated." Stephanie asked, incredulously, "It was too *complicated?*" The boy smiled sheepishly, and Stephanie moved on. The point was made. There was no need for further discussion. His excuse was inadequate, as well as improbable. Both the student and the teacher understood that he was unprepared for class, that she knew it, and that he was on notice to do his homework in the future.

Candid by nature, Stephanie was not reluctant to call students' bluffs. She said what she thought, which, in her dealings with students, made for authoritative moments. For example, during a science experiment, students were to fill containers with a set amount of water. Some groups were inattentive, and their experiments were not completed at the end of the class. When Stephanie told them they would have to repeat the lab after school, they asked if they could stay in at lunch instead. She replied, "I'm not going to spend my lunch" repeating this activity. One of the girls then said, "So *all* we have to do is put the water in?" Stephanie replied, "If that's *all*, then why didn't you do it?" The student gave a red-faced grin. Checkmate. Confrontational in a positive way, Stephanie is direct and clear without being unkind.

Her authoritative presence sometimes frees students to move on after an incident without losing face. For example, when Lamont and Marcus were squabbling before lunch, Lamont told Stephanie, "My dad told me to tell you" if Marcus bothered him. Stephanie listened to both boys, validated their concerns, and sent them—together—out to lunch. Her intervention was minimal. Mostly she lent her presence and affirmation to the situation. Before resuming their friendship, the boys needed to register their complaints with a grown-up; Stephanie filled the bill.

Some of the quieter, more subtle violations she also addressed with sensitivity and skill. She did not even pause for breath as she confiscated a student's beeper, proceeding through her lesson without a noisy confrontation. Interestingly, the students did not argue with her, accepting her right to take contraband from them. In fact, they called on her to mediate their

Gender Dynamics: Powerlessness and Inflexibility

Women face particular challenges in converting any theoretical power into actual authority. Insufficient authority to fulfill responsibilities leads to a feeling of powerlessness that can attract additional confrontation. Powerlessness, in turn, engenders certain kinds of inflexible behaviors that are rooted in fear and frustration. As a result, some teachers can bunker down in their classrooms, paying inordinate attention to inconsequential details or handing down arbitrary edicts on classroom practice. Sociologist Rosabeth Moss Kanter explained, "When people are rendered powerless in the larger arena, they may tend to concentrate their power needs on those over whom they have even a modicum of authority" in an image of the "old-maid schoolteacher" (1977, p. 189). That the image is feminine may be no accident. With few resources to draw on, women teachers, especially young ones, may find themselves relatively powerless and may respond in ways that exacerbate the original problem.

disputes and quarrels, expecting her to hear them out and render fair judgment. Stephanie explained, "I've had to learn to be mean. . . . Whether I'm the bad guy or not, they still like me." Significantly, she views herself as "mean" rather than authoritative. *Mean* has a much more negative connotation, one of unwarranted cruelty or selfishness. In fact, Stephanie's behavior is not cruel or selfish. It is appropriate and necessary. Apparently, by late winter her students have come to expect and generally appreciate this kind of authority in a teacher, and, as long as it is fair and delivered with some humor, it helps them by making the school environment predictable and safe. In any case, for Stephanie, this meanness is a learned emotion, a stance.

Pedagogy and Authority

In spite of these authoritative moments, Stephanie's classroom has a chaotic undertow. Her teaching practices may contribute to her classroom management problems. She came of age as a teacher in an era of cooperative learning, student-centered classrooms, portfolio assessment, and constructivism. The trend with these philosophies is to grant students more autonomy over their own education. By empowering students to make choices about writing topics and formats, books to read, schedules, and even evaluation criteria, the hope is to generate investment, inquiry skills, and relevance. Stephanie's emphasis on hands-on science, free reading time, journals, and a menu of independent math activities and games meant that students were often actively engaged in some learning activity.

Tips for New Teachers: Pedagogy and Classroom Management

Collectively, students in a class can be lively or raucous, subdued or disengaged. A contemplative mood may not lend itself to discussion, and buzzing excitement can impede test-taking. A teacher can use varying pedagogical approaches to manage the energy level in the class for different purposes.

To generate energy:

1. Use an animated, humorous tone

2. Offer group work or simulations

3. Direct questions to the class

4. Use rapid-fire questions

5. Open the environment

To absorb energy:

1. Use a flat, humorless tone

2. Use teacher-centered direct instruction, individual written work, or silent reading

3. Direct questions to individuals

4. Use slow questions with long wait times

5. Close the environment

The dark side of this engagement, of course, was that a fair amount of the walking around and talking had nothing to do with learning, and it was difficult for students to shift from independent time to more structured class time.

Effective student-centered learning requires tremendous teacher skill in orchestrating simultaneous worthwhile activities while monitoring student behavior and learning (Labbett, 1988). Otherwise, it is a sham that veils teacher abdication, withdrawal, or laziness. A fundamental charge of teaching—maintaining order—is enormously complicated when there are competing activities going on. Untrained eyes and ears may be hard pressed to track much of the movement and conversation, leaving lots of room for management problems. For an inexperienced teacher whose personal authority may be modest, attempting this kind of sophisticated pedagogy could be nightmarish.

Gender Dynamics: Student-Centered Teaching

"Child-centered teaching [is] part of this trap for women: It privileges the child over the teacher, thus making power in the classroom a contested and shifting property" (Acker, 1995, p. 123).

It is often easier and safer for a teacher to prepare a single lesson, stand in front of the students, and deliver it without interruption. The potential disadvantages of this kind of teacher-centered instruction are well known: student passivity, mechanical learning, and exclusion (Gardner, 1993). What may be less well known are the particular problems that new teachers are likely to have with the pedagogical styles that are currently in favor. Empowering students may be especially problematic for young women teachers. They need to acquire authority before they can—or can afford to—relinquish any.

Developing a sense of authority with students is not a finite project. It takes time and practice and maturity, and the goal may recede into the distance with each forward stride. However, authoritative management cannot wait. It is an urgent need for any new teacher, and particularly for a young woman. Although its absence may be less obvious, authoritative pedagogy is also an immediate concern for a new teacher. Of course, management and pedagogy are intertwined. Young women teachers, who may be particularly vulnerable to student challenge and defiance, wisely train their focus almost unerringly on these two facets of their job while they establish their authority.

CONCLUSION

Negotiating authoritative relationships with colleagues, parents, and students is a complicated business. Of all the dilemmas, however, perhaps none is more paradoxical than this: Effort taints authority. Authority is essential for effective teaching, it is not inherent in the role alone, and visible attempts to acquire it usually fail. This is bad news for new teachers. Young women, who typically are not perceived as authoritative, start with a deficit. They have to work hard to compensate for little structural support in being authoritative. However, this very effort undermines them. Part of being authoritative, then, becomes learning to act as if authority can be presumed: Authority taken for granted is often more convincing than authority clutched. As a result, learning to present an authoritative front requires careful crafting of a professional identity.

3

Helen
Professional Identity

[I did not understand fully] the role of the teacher and [the fact that I could] step into something that existed—a sense of authority that has been established from years and years of the profession and that I could tap into personally—I didn't realize until after I had started.

Helen

Like Stephanie, Helen was a second-year teacher still learning the ropes. She described an epiphany in which she discovered that she did not need to imagine herself struggling alone to invent from scratch some notion of what it means to be a teacher. Rather, she could assume her place in the gallery of teachers, like a fresh portrait securely surrounded by venerable ancestors. Their aura propelled her to a level of authority she might not have achieved on her own. The price, though, was a modicum of conformity.

For teachers, authority is both a cultural and functional necessity. People expect it, and it often works. However, placing oneself in the context of generations of teachers requires some adaptation. For young women teachers who lack authority on their own, this strategy may be particularly valuable. Association with distinguished colleagues can be a catalyst for credibility. A novice who is able to discern others' expectations of a teacher and then fulfill them saves herself some effort. Admittedly, compliance with traditional norms often implies some loss of individuality. New teachers may have to weigh their desire for individuality against their desire for authority. Achieving both is likely to be difficult, especially for a young woman teacher.

Meet the Teacher: Helen

Age: 24

Education: B.A. Liberal Studies

Professional Training: Provisional teaching credential

Number of Years Teaching: 2

Grade Level: 1st

Class Size: 20

Special Assignments: Bilingual Cantonese class

School Enrollment: 400

Schoolwide Eligibility for Subsidized Lunch: 50%

Schoolwide Student Ethnicity: 50% African American, 25% Asian, 25% Other

Schoolwide Achievement Scores Compared With National Average: Significantly below

For Helen, the choice was clear. Fresh from college, she was hired to teach a combination kindergarten and first-grade bilingual class in English and Cantonese. She was new to teaching, new to kindergarten, new to first grade, new to the school and district, and new to Cantonese. She would line up with the ancestors.

PRESENTATION OF SELF

Teaching is a kind of performance, and some teachers definitely work in character. A new teacher may adopt a persona for the school day. Like Patroclus dressed in Achilles' armor, she may borrow the trappings of others' authority in hopes of inspiring respect that she might not evoke on her own. In particular, new teachers may tailor their appearance, dress, title, and speech patterns to project a desired image.

Appearance and Dress

Physical size is often helpful in generating personal authority, and it is largely outside an individual's control. For young women, this reality can pose problems. On average, women are shorter than men. Particularly if

Cultural Dynamics: A Clothing Conundrum

Affluent parents who assume acceptance and lifelong participation of their children in the professional world may want the school to buffer their children from adult life. They may be happy with a teacher who dresses casually and puts a human face on the school bureaucracy. Parents who are less confident of their children's access to this adult professional world and its economic rewards may view school as a vital bridge to adult life. These parents may look to the teacher to dress more formally as a model and guide for the serious business of life preparation.

they are slender, it is easy for young women teachers to give the impression of using physical space tentatively, which tends to convey timidity rather than confidence. As a result of stature, weight, and voice pitch and volume, women often have a very different kind of physical presence than men (Bullough, 1989), and it is the male model that is associated with authority.

In contrast to the more fixed nature of physical size, new teachers have myriad choices about how to dress. Unfortunately, they face few unambiguously good options with regard to clothing. They may choose to dress up for work in hopes of garnering greater credibility. However, unlike some of their counterparts in other fields, if they dress up for school in an attempt to look like professionals and be taken seriously, they may find themselves overdressed for the elementary school environment. Dressing comfortably and casually might be more appropriate for someone who spends her days immersed in art projects, chalk, gardens, science experiments, lunch supervision, and field trips. In fact, undue concern about keeping clothes clean at the expense of engagement with students or materials looks less like professionalism than fastidiousness. Alternatively, overdressing may make the teacher appear like a fearful, threatened animal, puffing herself up to appear larger before predators. In any case, regardless of what they wear, new teachers are particularly vulnerable to criticism about their dress.

Helen recognized this dilemma and aligned herself with the more traditional style. She described a "uniform for the role of the teacher" characterized by "plain, nondescript" clothes and "a lot of coverage." She said, "I wouldn't come to work wearing jeans—not because I feel like there is a dress code, but for me, I would feel like I wasn't in character." For her, being "in character" meant looking like a teacher. She wore mid-calf-length skirts matched with sweaters and sensible, low-heeled shoes. Her work uniform was practical, sturdy, and no-nonsense. She looked like a teacher.

Gender Dynamics: Double Standards

The clothing of new women teachers may receive greater scrutiny than the clothing of their male peers. Tennis shoes that seem unremarkable on a male teacher may strike parents or administrators as too casual on a woman, especially if she is young. In responding to this double standard, a young woman teacher needs to make informed choices about her presentation of self, weighing practicality and principles with expectations and consequences.

Titles

In addition to appearance, new teachers have a range of choices about titles. It might be better if they did not. A printed title and surname may be the first piece of information that parents or students learn about a teacher. The surname may tell a tale. A surname with an ethnic ring might suggest a particular racial or cultural or religious background, although it may give no hint as to how fresh or distant that connection might be. Multiple last names, hyphenated or not, often suggest a desire to preserve multiple family names, often for cultural or philosophical reasons. For a woman, multiple last names may suggest a feminist inclination. In general, though, surnames are inherited through patriarchal or marriage lines rather than freely chosen. As a result, her surname may reveal less about a new teacher than the title she attaches to it.

Titles set the tone for interpersonal relations by establishing the degree of formality and respect in the relationship. Formal titles such as *Mr.*, *Mrs.*, *Miss*, or *Ms.* are a traditional, expected part of the teacher role in most school settings. While *Mr.* is an all-purpose formal title for men, women must choose to identify themselves by one of several possibilities, each with limitations. There is no neutral choice for a woman; each choice reveals significant information about her (Tannen, 1994). If she chooses to be addressed as *Mrs.*, she indicates that she is married or perhaps has been married in the past. Marriage connotes traditional household structure and the status of mainstream society. It suggests that the woman has adopted her husband's family name. It implies that she is a desirable person and clears her from the stigma of the stereotypical old maid schoolteacher (Acker, 1995).

If a woman teacher chooses to be known as *Miss*, she indicates that she is not married. In addition, she probably has not been married before, since divorced or widowed women rarely elect to be called *Miss*. While *Miss* may have a perky or youthful ring when used to describe a young woman, it may sound like a reproach or a sentence on an older one. In any case, *Miss* is a title that is out of favor with many young women. *Ms.* has some advantages over *Miss* or *Mrs.*, including obscuring marital status, but as an attempt to create a neutral title for women, *Ms.* has problems of its own. In some communities, it stands out. It can be hard to pronounce, drawing added emphasis. Most significantly, it can sound political or contentious. In a world where women's marital status has long been considered relevant information in the public domain, *Ms.* stakes the claim that *it's none of your business*. For better or worse, identifying herself as *Ms.* has ramifications for a young woman teacher, even in a freewheeling urban setting. In any case, a teacher's chosen title is an obvious, often printed, clue about social status, particularly for women.

In this group, four of the teachers elected to be addressed as *Ms.* None was married. The one married teacher, Julie, preferred to be called *Mrs.* Stephanie, like many other teachers in her school, preferred to have the students call her by her first name. She liked the implicit collaboration and equality of parallel names for teacher and students. As many of the teachers noted, however, it frequently does not matter what the teacher wants; in Paula's words, "They all call me *Mrs.* anyway." That title felt uncomfortable to some of the teachers, but it seemed somehow inevitable.

Speech Patterns

Like appearance and titles, speech patterns communicate a complicated message, of which content may be only a small part. New teachers who are conscious of the power of speech patterns face difficult choices about diction, tone, vocabulary, and sentence structure. Those who are less conscious of these choices are constrained by the impressions they may unwittingly send. Young adults may carry over into adulthood their youthful speech patterns, often with disappointing results. Young women, in particular, may be dismissed as vacuous if they are too proficient in the youth vernacular.

Another reason that a young woman's native voice is often ineffective in professional settings is that girls are socialized to speak in ways that are not perceived as authoritative (Gilligan, 1982; Tannen, 1990, 1994). Many girls learn to use tentative and circuitous speech patterns as part of a larger presentation of self as agreeable and pleasant. Strong opinions, clear directives, and commands often are not a part of the speech repertoire of young women, and the circuitous speech patterns they often use are sometimes assumed to signify uncertainty or weakness.

New teachers who seek authority face the additional complication of voice pitch. Most women's voices are pitched higher than men's, and a higher-pitched voice may seem anxious or tentative, even if it is not. Voice pitch can underscore the traditional incongruity between women and authority in a sensory way. Any voice is an asset and a limitation, but young

Gender Dynamics: Conversational Styles

Part of the culture of conversation among many women is self-depre-
cating candor and habitual apology. Some women willingly downplay their own authority and status in order to avoid appearing bossy
or insensitive. According to linguist Deborah Tannen, "Many of the rit-
uals typical of women's conversations depend on the goodwill of the
other not to take the self-abnegation literally and to restore the balance" (1994, p. 40). Combined with the general authority difficulties
that can plague young women teachers, this ritual is a risky, unilateral
strategy, leaving them vulnerable to appearing uncertain or incompe-
tent. Even in the world of elementary schools, which are full of women
teachers and mothers who may be familiar with this ritual, it may be
perceived as a signal of weakness.

women teachers' voices often pose particular problems for them. If combined with obvious youth or a slight frame or general tentativeness or a
transparent desire to please, a high-pitched voice simply completes the
impression of inexperience and vulnerability. It makes a young woman
teacher a likely target for opposition and aggression.

Straight Talk

Straight talk is many teachers' professional dialect. *Sit down. Take out
your homework. Raise your hand.* It is direct communication—often snappy,
terse directives—without vacillation or backpedaling or apology. Unfortunately, it is not the native tongue of many new teachers. Straight talk pre-
sumes thought-out opinions and denotes sufficient authority to speak
plainly, without fear of repercussions. However, young teachers may not
yet have carefully deliberated opinions. Women, even women in positions
of authority, often prefer to downplay that authority rather than invoke it
(Tannen, 1994). They often dislike the social discomfort of acknowledging
their authority through straight talk. As a result, young women teachers,
who may not have established opinions, may not feel or be authoritative,
and may be unwilling to invoke any authority they have, are often reluctant
to use straight talk with students, colleagues, or parents. In anticipating her
first Parent Night, Helen said:

I thought that I had to stand up and sell my program to all these parents. . . . *This is why it is okay that your child is in my room.* And Annette
from across the hall took me out to dinner before, and she was like,
No, this is what *you* want: You want *this* and *this* and *this* from the

Tips for New Teachers: Voice Inflection

Use voice inflection to reinforce your words and message. Your pitch should go up at the end of a sentence *only* if you are asking a question. As an exercise, repeat the following phrase emphasizing the underlined word. What are the nuances of each version?

The *assignment* is due tomorrow.

The assignment *is* due tomorrow.

The assignment is *due* tomorrow.

The assignment is due *tomorrow.*

parents. This is *our* program, these are *our* expectations, and this is what *you* need to do as a parent. And my whole perception of—not just that night—but the parent/teacher interaction is [that] I am telling them what *I* expect, not selling [my program] to them.

Helen's strategy seemed to work well in her bilingual Cantonese class populated by the children of Chinese immigrants eager to partake of American educational and economic opportunity. She might encounter more resistance in a class of students whose parents were disillusioned by the dearth of viable opportunity and suspicious of a new teacher with an agenda for them and their children. Nonetheless, Helen's account indicates that her professional identity included new speech patterns. Clearly not intuitive to her, these teacher speech patterns became an acquired skill, deliberately exercised.

Unfortunately for new teachers, here is the rub: If they do not use straight talk, they run the risk of being perceived as unclear or weak, but if they do use straight talk, they risk causing offense, provoking a backlash, or aggravating cultural misunderstandings. That kind of quandary is enough to make a person reluctant to say anything.

The Virtue of Reticence

In addition to learning to use straight talk effectively, young women teachers sometimes need to learn the value of reticence in professional contexts. For instance, Helen described feeling uneasy the day a mother unexpectedly visited her class and the students were boisterous and distracted after a visit to the school garden. Helen reported, "When they went out to recess or something, I wanted to say [to the mother], 'Oh, I'm so sorry. It is not usually like that.'" Helen said nothing, and in fact, the mother indicated that she was pleased that the students were outside visiting the garden. She thought it was a great activity. Had Helen confessed her reservations about the lesson, she would have called attention to concerns that this mother did not see.

Stephanie, also, learned this lesson in her first year of teaching. With the help of a more experienced colleague, she realized that sometimes engaging in conversation was damaging to her authority. She recounted:

> I had a student last year that was really, really bad. . . . He would throw chairs and get in fights every single day. He would swear at me and call me *bitch*, call me *white punk*, all the time, I mean all the time. At the beginning, I kept trying to reason with him, and Pamela, this great teacher said, Don't try to reason with him. That is what he wants you to do and you are giving him too much credit for his argument when you respond. And he would say stuff like, *That's not true*. And I would say, Yes, it is true. And he would be like, *No, it's not*. And I would say, Yes, you did that. And he would say, *No, I didn't*. Yes, you did. *No, I didn't*. And you get to this interplay which is not appropriate.

It was liberating for Stephanie to discover that she need not engage in pointless arguments. An authoritative teacher does not have to bicker this way. She knows what she knows, and she acts decisively based on that knowledge. Talk only weakens her position.

New teachers are often surprised to discover how much dress, appearance, titles, and speech patterns matter. They are important sources of authority. Of course, authority based on imitation and superficial appearance is more fragile than authority based on conviction and experience. It is a house built on sand. Even so, a house built on sand can provide shelter while a better foundation is prepared on firmer ground. New teachers, and young women in particular, need immediately viable strategies for being authoritative. As they make choices about their professional identity, they are wise to attend to the ways they present themselves.

PRESENTATION OF THE CLASSROOM

Another important component of professional identity comes from creating an environment that is professional, that facilitates productivity, that engages students, that reassures parents and administrators, and that meets expectations for what a classroom should look like. Unlike some other employees, teachers work in a public environment. Their primary workspace, the classroom, is also the students' work site. It is the area that

Gender Dynamics: Feminine Authority

Mothers often epitomize a nurturing, feminine kind of authority, and are granted a certain respect and honor for their influential role in raising children. However, this respect is double-edged. Caring for children is both joyful and tedious, rewarding and messy, and in a strictly rational accounting, it carries not only no financial remuneration but often penalties and personal sacrifice. Though mothers are powerful people in the eyes of their young children, they control no critical resources that would make them seem powerful to other adults (Pfeffer & Salancik, 1978). Their work is ordinary. As a result, this more feminine brand of authority becomes linked with low-status work and poor compensation (Biklen, 1993). The roles for women that carry lucrative salaries, influence over adults, and respect in the public sphere are more likely to be roles that historically have been occupied by men and for which rewards are assigned to behavior that resembles traditional authority (Kanter, 1977).

parents see—not only on carefully staged Parent Nights but also when they drop off or pick up their children. It is the space administrators see when they conduct formal evaluations as well as when they happen to walk by any day of the school year. If the classroom is chaotic, congested, disorderly, or even just cluttered, everyone knows. If it is carefully organized, aesthetic, colorful, and engaging, everyone also knows. Whether it is truly a classroom of her own or not, this physical environment is an extension of the teacher's professional identity, and it is worth her attention.

Managing Space

Managing the classroom environment can be time-consuming, expensive, and laborious. Whatever it is, it is not trivial. While all teachers face this issue, expectations for a neat and inviting classroom may be particularly high for women. A new teacher who imagines that her college education should excuse her from bulletin board decorating may be in for a rude awakening. Since her mastery of teaching is likely to be tenuous, her classroom had better inspire confidence.

Significantly, many of the newest teachers find themselves traveling among different classrooms for the first few years. They share rooms with other teachers, switching either during preparation periods or during off-track schedules at year-round schools. Ideally, every teacher would have her own room, but in many schools there simply are not enough to go around. Someone has to rove. Roving undermines a teacher's sense of professional identity by separating her from control of the physical work space.

Helen was well aware of the importance of the classroom as a window on her professional identity. She explained, "It's my role and my job to organize this environment." She knew that teaching was not just about curriculum and pedagogy; it was also about presentation and orchestration. Helen discovered early on that with "an air of confidence" about her and good classroom structure, the children and their parents relaxed, convinced that they were in good hands. She noted:

> [Parents] expect me to act like a teacher. I mean, they expect homework to come home of a certain nature, they expect there to be spelling tests, they expect there to be parties on certain days, they expect me to *be* there. I watched them watch me interact with their children in the beginning of the year, and it seemed like as soon as they realized that their children are happy and that I am kind and patient, then they are happy.

Helen posted a weekly lesson plan chart on her file cabinet. It listed each week's activities and the general curricular goals they addressed. By district mandate, Helen had to submit lesson plans in advance, but she went beyond the minimal requirements. Instead of handwritten scrawl intelligible only to herself, she submitted a computer-generated chart that was also suitable for display in her classroom. With one stroke, she fulfilled evaluation requirements and provided an overview for parents or others who might drop in unexpectedly. Additionally, each week Helen put together a homework packet of worksheets and lined writing paper along with a cover sheet listing the topics of the week, spelling words, upcoming tests, and other ongoing activities. It communicated with the parents so that they would have the understanding and resources to reinforce school activities at home.

Similarly, Helen created a poster every few weeks that listed the highlights of the month. The posters covered the ceiling, and the children could look at them any time to see how much they had done. Perhaps more important, these posters were a public relations triumph: colorful and informative, they created a sense of efficiency, rigor, and progress. They were a masterful pre-emptive strike against anyone who might challenge Helen's instructional program. Her classroom setup created the impression of a teacher who was organized and thorough. This anticipatory groundwork in establishing credibility is important in deterring or responding to challenges.

Managing Curriculum

In addition to creating a good impression, effective organization of the classroom also builds confidence and allows for more sophisticated curriculum and pedagogy. Part of a young teacher's skillful presentation is simply having the confidence and experience to stand back and let others see what she has wrought. Classroom time devoted to the simultaneous independent activities that are common in elementary schools can be particularly unnerving for a teacher under observation. Helen said that she would have felt uncomfortable the previous year if the principal had walked in on one of these "controlled chaos" lessons. In this second year of teaching, Helen was not worried and said, "Now I'm organized, I'm structured, and I can explain why each thing is happening." She had her lesson plan chart, specific workstations, and assigned teams to back her up. She also was more familiar this year with stock defenses of her program. Knowing that she can talk the talk of educational rationales, Helen was less concerned about the inevitable student noise and motion. In this case, her management of curriculum and pedagogy was rooted in greater understanding and confidence.

However, that is not always the case. For example, in Helen's district there was increased attention to science as part of the elementary curriculum, and Helen was working on strengthening her science program. She was also managing impressions about it. Her classroom included a bulletin board entitled "Super Science" and similar stickers that she distributed after a science activity. She reported that she taught science three times a week and science appeared on her weekly lesson plan and on the monthly summary charts. The classroom windowsills were filled with sprouting peanuts, bulbs, and vegetable seedlings. Science was broadly conceived in Helen's room, though. It included illustrating a poem about the rain forest and blending peanuts into peanut butter. This overlap with Language Arts and Social Studies could be justified as interdisciplinary or thematic teaching. However, at some point, those terms may become smoke screens for tangential science instruction.

For young women teachers, this issue may be particularly relevant. A Liberal Studies major in college, Helen had taken a small number of math or science classes to fulfill her degree requirements. Although she said that she felt comfortable teaching science, her preparation was modest, at best. With regard to science, this thin preparation is disproportionately a problem for women (American Association of University Women Educational Foundation [AAUWEF], 1992). Helen acknowledged that she would like to teach more science, and she hoped to use the annual district science fair as an opportunity. This year, she sent home instructions on the science fair so that interested families could participate, but there was no in-class support. In the future, she hoped to do one or more in-class projects.

Sensibly, Helen added new curriculum incrementally. She began with the subjects that get the most attention in the primary grades: literacy and numeracy. Science would have to come later. Unfortunately, for some elementary teachers, later never arrives. They may skirt substantive science instruction by focusing on maintaining bulletin boards and dreaming up related Language Arts projects. While these activities shape impressions and can be important and useful, they are a poor substitute for science curriculum and pedagogy.

Managing Impressions

Part of the successful presentation of the classroom environment is managing interactions with the various official evaluators. In a bilingual class like Helen's, those evaluators include the district staff who verify compliance with the myriad regulations that govern bilingual education. During her first year, when Helen was assigned a combined kindergarten and first grade bilingual class, she agreed to enroll simultaneously in a district-sponsored Cantonese program two nights a week. As the teacher of a bilingual class, she was supposed to provide instruction in both English and Cantonese with the assistance of a Cantonese-speaking instructional aide. From the beginning, this plan did not work. The promised aide spoke Mandarin, not Cantonese, and because of a personality conflict, she did not work in Helen's classroom for long. Helen pretended, at least on evaluation days, to be offering instruction in two languages. She included pages of Chinese writing in her lesson plans. But she taught only in English.

This year, Helen decided to make some changes. She informed her principal that she would no longer participate in the bilingual teacher-in-training program. She dropped out of the Cantonese class. And she stopped feigning compliance for the bilingual evaluators. Helen explained, "I decided not to pretend [to be in compliance] because of the extra work involved, and philosophically, at this point, I don't feel like it is the right thing to do to pretend." She conceded that the general hiring climate in the state gave her the confidence to make these changes because class-size reduction had created a shortage of qualified teachers. Even in the event that her district did not rehire her, she would be unlikely to be unemployed if she wanted to teach. However, this decision had painful consequences for Helen. She explained that it "creates that dichotomy of wanting to be the perfect little student girl person who is doing everything just great and then also wanting to stand up and say, 'No, I am taking a stand.'" Her own sense of integrity and growing professional confidence enable Helen to act on her reservations.

The sequence of events leading to this set of circumstances is disturbingly logical. Helen needed a job. She was offered one for which she was fundamentally unqualified. Promised help fell through. Evaluators were satisfied with cursory evidence like paper lesson plans. Helen was hungry for positive feedback. She tried to coax it from evaluators by being agreeable and pleasant, telling them what they wanted to hear about her program. The deception began innocently enough, but it grew. When the end came, Helen explained, "I was sort of frustrated because I wanted a positive evaluation. But I would like to have a genuine positive evaluation, not that [the evaluator] walks in and sees Chinese handwriting on the walls and thinks that they are learning Chinese in here when they are not." Helen discovered the downside of managing others' impressions too well. If the disparity between image and reality is too great, the teacher does not come across as credible; she comes across as duplicitous.

Good teaching possesses a quality of confidence and control. It is rare in a new teacher, who is hard-pressed to control the many, many coincident demands of the job. It may be particularly rare in a young woman teacher, whose presentation of self—both deliberate and involuntary—can undermine even her best efforts. To the degree that a new teacher can control and shape the presentation of her classroom, she increases both her chances of teaching well and her chances of being perceived by others as teaching well.

PRESENTATION OF EMOTIONS

In addition to managing the classroom environment, a new teacher must learn to manage her own emotions. Teaching is emotional work, crowded with complex and overlapping relationships. New teachers, who may attract more than their fair share of challenging student behavior, must train themselves to respond calmly and firmly. The wisest will recognize inappropriate student behavior as a part of the job and steel themselves against being freshly offended or angry by students' reflexive defiance, recalcitrance, or outright insubordination. A teacher who cannot stop the emotional drain of routine incidents will soon be flattened by the juggernaut of fatigue and frustration. Experienced teachers come to know that although some behavior is calculated, much of the tiresome and peevish behavior their students exhibit is truly impulsive. Managing emotions helps the teacher monitor her own impulsive and calculated behavior in the interests of learning.

Anger

Anger is a problematic emotion for new teachers. Inevitably, it arises in teaching, and almost as inevitably, it creates quandaries, particularly for young women. Direct anger is often considered unseemly in girls, and young women are often seasoned experts at suppressing it (Pipher, 1994). When they do become angry, some have difficulty expressing that anger at all, especially in a controlled way. It sometimes erupts as tears, which may

Tips for New Teachers: Nonverbal Communication

Explicitly teach your students to recognize your emotions, and learn to communicate them with nonverbal cues. Spend two minutes the first week of school explaining that when you stand in a certain corner or switch off the lights momentarily or hold up two fingers or stand with your hands on your hips, you are losing patience and they need to pay attention immediately. There is no guarantee the students will do exactly as you wish, but the odds increase if they understand your warning signals.

seem unprofessional, or in shouting, which may seem ineffective and embarrassing. In either of those cases, the young woman teacher appears weak and loses face (Measor, 1985).

Conversely, anger has serviceable functions that may benefit new teachers, and young women in particular. Anger that is specific and justified can be a productive tool in interactions with students and colleagues. It has appropriate and strategic uses, as in defending someone's rights, communicating displeasure, or escalating a long-standing confrontation. In fact, a public showdown can help deter future problems and convince colleagues and students alike that the teacher is capable of and willing to engage in conflict when necessary.

Helen discovered the value of strategic anger when she was a student teacher. One day when the master teacher left the room, the students began acting out. The situation deteriorated until Helen reached a breaking point and thought to herself, "No. Stop. I am going to get things back together." She did, calming the students and guiding them back to the lesson. When the master teacher returned, Helen was still somewhat agitated. Helen reported that her master teacher said, "That's it. I see the fire in your eyes! That is good." The master teacher recognized what Helen did not have enough experience to know: Anger can be a powerful motivator and impetus for improvement.

Part of the successful use of anger is capitalizing on the moment. Helen's master teacher advised her that when she does get angry, she should "take advantage of the situation because that is one moment when [she is] going to have everyone's attention. . . . Don't give it away." In other words, anger is not by definition something to be ashamed of or quickly dismiss, as young women may be socialized to believe. Instead, it is part of the repertoire of strategies a teacher can use to get her students' attention.

Over time, Helen also learned to use dramatic anger to her advantage. She found that she could detach her inner emotions from the external display. "I could get angry, but I didn't *feel* angry," she admitted. Clearly, this strategy has some disadvantages. Decoupling emotions and behavior may allow a teacher to disengage from her work. Furthermore, it may diminish the impact of her real episodes of anger. However, putting on the mask of anger has some advantages. Anger takes a physical and psychological toll. It creates tensions and stresses that linger well after the incident has passed. Acting reduces this physical toll. Furthermore, students need to recognize a teacher's anger in order for it to be effective for her. If she is seething inside but the class is oblivious, her anger buys her nothing but stress and aggravation. Both teacher and students may need some training in communicating emotions accurately. Acting may facilitate that kind of practice when the stakes are not too high.

Helen used this approach when a boy pushed another child into her. Atypically, she raised her voice. Suddenly everyone in the class was listening. In discussing the incident later, Helen explained, "Sometimes I feel like I was too harsh on him . . . but at the same time, it is also sort of a general statement to everyone: don't push people." Helen recognized early on that anger is not her enemy. It can be a force to be harnessed. To the degree that a new teacher can learn to master her anger, it can work for her.

Frustration

Like anger, frustration is inherent to teaching. New teachers may be particularly prone to it on account of the combination of difficult teaching circumstances and limited supporting resources that they often face. Uncontrolled, their frustration has the potential to undermine them. Helen acknowledged, "You take it personally when kids are doing whatever they are doing. You see that as a reflection of yourself directly." She found that over time, she was able to be more philosophical about student behavior that frustrated her. She explained:

> Once you are a teacher, you are a teacher and kids react to you as a teacher and not to you-the-person. You-the-person definitely shines through and is who you are, but you are always the teacher, so a lot of those reactions you get are just reactions to teachers.

In other words, Helen was learning to externalize student behavior, to release herself from the need to be hurt or angry if they were less than model citizens. She was developing thicker skin, for better and worse. Like other strategies for managing emotions, this one has mixed results. It frees teachers from feeling personally affronted every time a student misbehaves. On the other hand, it may allow a teacher to disconnect herself from negative student behavior so much that she fails to see ways that she may provoke, fail to deter, or simply countenance inappropriate behavior. In any event, some emotional detachment is likely to reduce the frustration that can be part of teaching, especially for novices.

Worth Discussing: Standard Procedures

Within a week, you discover two separate incidents of cheating (or name-calling or vandalism or fighting) in class. You spend precious time and energy anguishing over confronting the student, informing the parents, and determining an appropriate response. You want to be fair and to consider each incident separately, but you have other pressing demands on your time. What are the advantages and disadvantages of categorical responses to negative or harmful student behavior? What about for positive or helpful student behavior?

Recurring issues can be frustrating, especially if a new teacher does not recognize them as part of a pattern. A wise teacher does not have to start from scratch every time a library book gets lost or curriculum generates controversy. She comes to know the patterns of school life and organizes her responses accordingly. The best teachers learn to acknowledge unique features while asserting commonalities. Like Martha Nussbaum's good navigator, she "does not go by the rule book; and she is prepared to deal with what she has not seen before. But she knows, too, how to use what she has seen; she does not pretend that she has never been on a boat before" (Nussbaum, 1990, p. 75). New teachers effectively have not been on the boat before. However, if they are attentive to recurring categories of behavior or incidents, they can help manage their frustration.

Perhaps the greatest benefit of Helen's approach to frustration is that it sets more reasonable expectations than idealistic new teachers might. They may imagine that they will be able to create an environment where conflict is infrequent or unnecessary. Helen learned to see past those illusions. In terms of her confrontations with students, she explained:

> The thing that I have to remember is that it never ends. It literally never ends. You can't think that if [you] do this ten times then they will stop doing it. They are always going to be testing, so I need to be in a state of mind where that is okay. . . . It is like upholding a standard but not getting angry when it continually gets challenged.

For many new teachers, this kind of thinking represents a dramatic re-orientation. It requires making peace with conflict and can be a beginning of wisdom.

Fear

Another emotion new teachers have to confront is fear. That a teacher might be afraid may be surprising. After all, a teacher is the lone adult in a room full of children or young people. An elementary teacher has adult status, generally larger physical size, more education, greater life experience, and official state or district endorsement to be in charge. What's to fear in the classroom?

The answers vary. For a new teacher, they include the fear that the students will not obey her, that parents will challenge her, that she will be exposed as barely competent, that she will make mistakes in public, that colleagues will undermine her, that she will have to control a crowd, or that she will lose control. Helen described her own fears:

> I used to be so nervous when I stood in front of the class that I had to hang on to the cart so that I wouldn't fall over because my autonomic nervous system would shut off. I would start to tip because I was so nervous. I would write on the board, and I would leave the last letter off of words because everything was shutting down.

Helen's fear impaired her ability to think clearly. Unchecked, it would certainly constrain her effectiveness as a teacher. Fortunately, teachers get lots of opportunities to practice in front of students. On another occasion when students were acting up, Helen said, "I remember turning around and facing the blackboard and thinking to myself, *You are the adult, you can't leave*, which is exactly what I wanted to do." Like most other teachers who last through induction, Helen found that her fears subsided over time. New teachers may find this initial stage fright particularly daunting. As they master it, they strengthen their authority in the classroom.

There is another, more insidious fear that can shadow teachers. It is the fear of physical danger and violence. Students sometimes have access to weapons and other tantalizing implements that follow them to school. Off-campus feuds, many with intense geographic or ethnic rivalries, may seep under the school's cyclone fence. Sometimes they live in the enflamed hearts of the students whose craving for respect may be tinged with acts of bravado or hostility. Other times, fear comes embodied in older siblings, cousins, and parents who linger around campus. The fear is compounded if it involves the teacher directly, for instance if she evokes ire through some disciplinary measure or grade. For women in general, the specter of violence can rarely be banished (Tannen, 1994), and for young women teachers, it may be a constant undercurrent. In classroom interactions, there may be "a specifically sexual element to the challenge [that gains] its point from being addressed to a woman teacher" (Measor, 1985, p. 74). Women may be perceived as easy targets for verbal attacks and defiance, as well as physical aggression. Whether real or implied or imagined, fear is not an irrational emotion in a teacher. It is one that must be controlled—both by individuals and by the school community—or it can be utterly debilitating.

Courage

Courage is a necessary part of a teacher's makeup (Sockett, 1993). Authoritative teaching requires a certain resolve and tenacity. It demands firmness, and firmness requires courage. Helen described herself as "someone who wants to create harmony and have everyone get along." However, she discovered that she had to develop a reserve of "courage to be firm" in creating an environment where all students could learn. Helen explained, "There is such a desire to want the kids to like you and accept you, and you want to do the right thing for them." As she came to understand, there is often a conflict between being liked and doing right. Over time, she decided, "When I am firm with the kids it is not necessarily hurting them." The implication of her phrasing—that firmness is hurtful—may be characteristically feminine. It is a revelation to her that courage to be firm might be in everyone's best interests. As Helen explained, it is preferable to the inevitable alternative:

> In a way, gently over time—but firmly—say [to students], "These are the parameters, this is appropriate behavior, and if you go off here, I am going to tell you so that you can come back" instead of just letting [them] go, go, go, and then flipping out and [saying], "You're suspended," and the kid is like, *Well, what happened?*

This kind of courage to be firm can help the students with gradual, consistent feedback that may defuse disruptive or dangerous outbursts. It can also help the teacher. Regular, calm encounters can relieve the teacher's frustration in small increments so that her anger does not boil over in an uncontrolled rage. As well, by creating a predictable and secure environment, she structures a situation where learning can happen. To do otherwise would be lax and wasteful. It is not always instinctive to new teachers that firmness can be kindness, but it is a lesson that may be particularly crucial for them to learn.

Emotions are part of good teaching. They are also part of bad teaching. Unfortunately, there are few hard and fast rules to govern their use. Sometimes a soft word, a raised eyebrow, the mere hint of a frown or smile is sufficient to achieve the desired result. Other times, however, a raised voiced, pointed vocabulary, or the threat of repercussions is needed. Often it is the element of surprise that makes a style effective. A teacher who rarely raises her voice may command great attention on the occasion when she does. A naturally boisterous teacher may find that whispering is particularly effective. A wise teacher will develop a range of emotions, stances, techniques, styles, and voices to mix and match as different needs arise.

New teachers, who may be unaccustomed to thinking of teaching as performance art and of communication as strategic, may be ill at ease with these calculations. Some may find it difficult to go from one style to another, to pull off a performance in a style not their own. They may be reluctant to manufacture emotions or uncomfortable with bluster. Most damaging, some may rely on a single presentation of self—often soft-spoken and polite—for so long that the strain breaks them. It is better for them to learn to use emotions to their advantage and in the service of educational aims.

PROFESSIONAL AND PERSONAL

A sense of professional identity includes many components: dress, speech, classroom presentation, and emotional stance, among others. There are some notable omissions, however. What is not included in a professional identity is revealing. Like employees in other professions, some teachers find that they prefer to have their professional and personal lives be distinct and separate. Some deliberately choose long commutes or at least find consolation in this physical space between home and work. This distance decreases the chance that they will run into students or parents at movie theaters, in grocery stores, or in restaurants. Helen explained, "I have thought a lot about moving [closer to school] because it would certainly be more convenient, but I really feel like when I go across the bridge . . . that I am sort of going back to a different me, and that helps." Helen liked the freedom of having a teacher life and a civilian life, and at present, she is not interested in working at the school half a block from her home because then she "would always have to be 'on.'" The convenience of proximity could not compensate for the loss of freedom.

A known personal life can compromise a teacher's professional image. It pierces the shield of privacy that allows for a professional identity in the first place. A personal life that is fluid or prone to significant revisions is likely to inspire curiosity in others. As well, young women teachers, like their male colleagues, are often forming key relationships during these early professional years, and may prefer to protect those early ties from the scrutiny of their school communities. For young women teachers, general awareness of romantic relationships can undermine their authority at school by calling attention to them as sexual beings. Young women teachers seem most willing to bring their personal and private lives together if their private lives are stable, official, and mainstream.

The moral overtones of teaching can complicate the matter of public and private lives. There were features of the teachers' private lives that seemed to them inconsistent with their public roles. For instance, Julie (see Chapter 7) worked for a year in a small town where she routinely ran into students at Wal-Mart and other public places. She said, "[I] always worried about who I might see," sometimes prompting her to think, "I can't wear this [outfit]." Similarly, Paula (see Chapter 4) worked briefly in a small town and felt "nervous about having [her] personal life" exposed. She did not want to see students or parents when she was "going out for a beer with a friend on a Friday night." Karen (see Chapter 6) lived away from her school because she believed that otherwise teaching would "seep into all the corners of [her] life." Additionally, she did not want her students to know that she lived with her fiancé. According to Karen, she did not want to give the impression, "Yeah, we're shacked up, and it's great." She believed this "porthole into [her] personal life" might undermine her professional identity. A separation protected each from the other.

Of course, teachers, like many other people, cannot always live exactly where they might choose. Some communities are utterly unaffordable for a teacher without another significant source of income. However, some teachers feel strongly about integrating their professional and personal lives as much as possible. Some live in the communities where they teach and seek out opportunities to interact with students outside of school time. This kind of proximity affords opportunities to visit students' homes for dinner, attend religious occasions, bump into students and parents informally around town, and perhaps most significantly, be perceived as and become a neighborhood insider. This familiarity can produce a level of trust between the teacher and community members that can be the foundation of widespread authority for that teacher. It requires a level of confidence and comfort with oneself and with the community, though. There are successful teachers who integrate their personal and professional lives, and successful ones who do not. However, for some teachers, the advantages of living outside the school community outweigh the advantages of living within it.

CONCLUSION

Authoritative teaching is predicated on a clear sense of professional identity. For new teachers, crafting and finessing that identity is a particularly daunting undertaking. For some, the complex task of developing an adult persona coincides with the urgent need for a coherent professional self. Young women teachers frequently join a new profession at the same time as they form key personal relationships, confront dilemmas about their role in society, and try to develop confidence and competence in their professional lives. This significant amount of turmoil is merely the backdrop to the demands of full-time daily performance as a teacher. Given a combination of conscious choices and involuntary realities, new teachers shoulder a heavy load. The school culture may ease or add to their burden.

4 Paula

School Culture

Teachers are workers, teaching is work, and the school is a workplace.

R. W. Connell

Paula is the eldest of the teachers in this study and has commensurately more life experience. She has lived in China and Japan, worked as a long-term substitute, and taught in both urban and more rural settings. In spite of her general confidence, optimism, and desire to do good, teaching leaves her feeling sometimes insecure, resentful, and alienated. The culture of the school where she works, and the cultures of schools in general, may help explain the gap between her hopes and her reality.

Ideally, schools would be places of equity and respect, of rigor and reflection. A significant body of evidence asserts that schools are not meeting this ideal for students (AAUWEF, 1992; Delpit, 1995; Ladson-Billings, 1994; Orenstein, 1994; Paley, 1979; Sizer, 1984). Unfortunately, one need look no farther than the experience of the newest members of the teaching force to find that many schools are not places where students *or* teachers can function well. For new teachers who seek attention, encouragement, and feedback, the culture of schools is often disenchanting.

There is a misconception about teaching that can foster unrealistic—though commendable—expectations. It begins with the notion that teaching is a helping profession, and that, by extension, schools must be supportive environments where teachers are helped to help others. As well, many elementary schools are staffed almost entirely by women, and their motivation for choosing this work is often attributed to selflessness and service. Further, many women prefer participatory leadership styles and less hierarchical work relationships (Gilligan, 1982; Kanter, 1977; Robertson, 1992; Tannen, 1994).

Age: 30

Education: B.A. in Art

Professional Training: Teaching credential

Number of Years Teaching: 3½

Other Work Experience: Teacher of English in China and Japan

Grade Level: K–6

Class Size: Variable

Special Assignments: Release teacher, multigrade classes, sheltered instruction

School Enrollment: 500

Schoolwide Eligibility for Subsidized Lunch: 90%

Schoolwide Student Ethnicity: 70% Latino, 20% African American, 10% Other

Schoolwide Achievement Scores Compared With National Average: Significantly below

Given this information, one might conclude that schools should be nurturing places where the lofty goal of education strips any contentious details of their power to frustrate or divide. New teachers may be surprised to discover that their workplace culture is no less mired in mundane conflicts than any office, factory, or business. If teachers are workers, then many of the concerns of other types of employees—such as working conditions and salary—are well within their purview. If teaching is work, then presumably there are requisite skills that can be learned and demonstrated. If the school is a workplace, then perhaps it is subject to the same problems that characterize other places of employment, including fads and cycles, pressure to routinize behavior, complex and competing incentives, rivalries and collusion, and subcultures of self-interest and insubordination.

Teaching is not exempt from these concerns, even if its purposes are altruistic. As a result, concern for the well-being of a child is not necessarily more appropriate in a teacher than concern about class assignments or resource allocation. It is this demythologizing of school culture that may be most jarring to new teachers. Culture is complex and has many possible incarnations. For purposes of considering the experience of new teachers, this chapter will address three facets of school culture: the school environment, assignments, and isolation and connection.

THE SCHOOL ENVIRONMENT

Relentlessly gray, black, and tan, Paula's school is situated in an urban neighborhood adjacent to a freeway, the light rail, and a major sports venue. As at many urban schools, there is no lawn and little greenery of any kind. The schoolyard is all blacktop, and the few jungle gyms were soon to be removed to make room for portable classrooms. These classrooms would provide needed instructional space, but they would consume scarce playground area in a neighborhood with few outdoor resources for children. Paula found these trade-offs painful. Hers was not an environment of plenty.

The School Garden

One bright spot for her was the school garden, a project she organized. On the blacktop, a corps of volunteers recently had built several planter boxes out of fresh, new wood. Ideally, this garden would give the children hands-on experience with the growing cycle, a small-scale understanding of agriculture, and a sense of investment in their school. An admirable idea, the implementation was somewhat disappointing. A young peach tree planted in a wine barrel was upended over a weekend. Student teachers offered to build a protective wall around the boxes and paint a mural on it, but they ended up being too overwhelmed to follow through.

The bins were partially full of soil, supporting a little lettuce gone to seed, some drooping bulbs, a few weeds, and a shriveled stalk of corn. The plants were improbable tenants, particularly given that there was no nearby water source. On a day in late May, two weeks before school would end for the summer, Paula recruited some students at recess to help her plant some donated tomato and bell pepper seedlings. The students enthusiastically pulled on gardening gloves and began turning the soil with trowels. The soil was dry, so a couple of students trekked to the nearest classroom with a bucket to fetch some water. Paula explained to the students that anyone who would water and weed the garden over the summer could harvest the vegetables. None of the students expressed interest. Several would be spending the summer in Mexico, and a few others said that they had gardens at home. The harvest is a remote reward with obvious and significant impediments.

A bountiful crop is not the only measure of success. Paula's goal had been to get the planter boxes built. She succeeded, and this patch of the yard

> ### Tips for New Teachers: Time and Task Management
>
> "As a new faculty member, you need to find ways to manage your time and tasks efficiently (doing things right), *and* to control what you put on your plate in the first place (doing the right things). If you do not do both, all the effort you put into your professional work will be for naught: you will simply burn out, and in the process endanger your career and your relationships with the people you care about most" (Reis, 1997, p. 245).

was marked off and prepared for future plantings. In addition, the students obviously enjoyed working with their hands outdoors in the sun for a few minutes. The garden is tangible evidence of external support and generosity. The boxes are new and semi-permanent resources for the school. While not currently set up to support the garden, the school might be at some point in the future.

However, the garden is part hope, part wish. It is too late in the year, both academic and calendar, for this kind of planting. Inadequate soil preparation, insufficient knowledge of planting, and nebulous ownership handicapped the project from the start. Worse, there is no plan for long-term viability. Without a water source, the garden is a sham. As well, it requires a certain optimism to invest much in an outdoor garden on a public site that is vacant at nights and on weekends. It relies for survival on goodwill and luck. By the next week, half the plants were missing and the remaining ones were withered. Laboring in obscurity, relying on chance and hope, and leaving the harvest to some unknown time and person are not typically the strategies of authoritative people. Even among teachers, who live with these conditions more than many people, Paula's charge stands out as frustrating.

Furthermore, the cost of coordinating the school garden project is not small for Paula. It damages her incipient authority to be in charge of a project that is not important enough to the school administration to support with timely resources. For new teachers, and young women in particular, this kind of leadership opportunity can be a particularly unfruitful trap. Their modest authority makes acquiring resources and support difficult, inadequate resources and support make failure probable, and perceived failure diminishes future authority. If an environment fosters the routine misappropriation and misapplication of people and resources, it cannot support a positive work culture, particularly for new employees who inevitably will be among the first and most frequent to be caught in its unproductive gears.

Tips for New Teachers: Special Assignments

Before accepting a special assignment, be sure you can answer the following questions:

1. What is the final goal or product (a yearbook, a new sports program, a task force)? Is it one-time or ongoing? How long might you have this assignment?

2. What resources are needed and available to support this assignment?

3. What compensation (stipend, reduced teaching load) is offered?

4. If this assignment has been done before, what issues or conflicts have arisen in the past? How have they been resolved?

5. If this assignment is new, why is it being added? Who are the key proponents? Are there opponents? What potential problems or conflicts can you foresee?

6. How would this assignment affect your core teaching responsibilities? Career goals? Personal life?

Resources

As the garden example demonstrates, part of the culture of the school environment is the constant struggle over insufficient resources. There is never enough of almost anything essential or desirable. When resources are scarce, there is competition, infighting, resentment, and jealousy that undermine a positive and healthy work culture. To compound this problem, the people with the least status in an organization often get the dregs of distributed reserves and commodities.

Resources sometimes are elusive for new teachers, in part because there is a perverse logic to them that new people are unlikely to follow. For instance, when Stephanie was hired, she asked her principal if an unused piano could be moved upstairs to her classroom. The principal seemed willing but stumped by the logistics, and nothing was done. Stephanie took her class to the auditorium every week, and the office secretary was so bothered by the noise that *she* lobbied the principal to move a piano upstairs. Problem solved.

Teachers may be surprised by their dependence on a complex network of coworkers for needed resources. This reality of bureaucratic life may be particularly unsettling for new teachers because their own domains are often small and peripheral, leaving them at a disadvantage when negotiating with others. In the game of resource distribution, new teachers are pit-

> ### Age Dynamics: Seniority Problems
>
> On account of their double lack of seniority, teachers who are both new and young may find that they have the least desirable assignments and facilities, and they may have a particularly difficult time getting access to the resources they need to do their jobs. These teachers bear a significant amount of the compression during lean times because they have little bargaining power and insufficient experience to anticipate needs or stockpile available materials.

ted against colleagues whose support and camaraderie they may be eager to cultivate. In the grand scheme, sacrificing needed resources for collegial goodwill—or at least the absence of ill will—may strike some teachers as reasonable. These kinds of harmful concessions signal a culture that is not productive, and they are likely to be disproportionately harmful to the newest teachers.

Broken Windows

The school culture inevitably is influenced by the environment. Paula's school was not well maintained. According to her, all of the old portable classrooms leaked. The previous year, one had a hole in the ceiling that took months to get fixed, a delay that Paula found disrespectful to the students. At Stephanie's school, the teachers' lounge was dirty and embarrassing to her. It was a small room, and most of it was designated as storage space. The refrigerator did not work. While the aging of urban schools may not be surprising, the degree of deterioration and complacency about repair and maintenance may be. More significantly, the effect of this environment on new teachers, perhaps young women in particular, may not be obvious.

Researchers James Wilson and George Kelling, in their analysis of police and neighborhood safety, found that the condition of public spaces and environments had powerful effects on people's perception of their own safety. They asserted that "if a window in a building is broken *and is left unrepaired,* all the rest of the windows will soon be broken" and that "untended property" seemed to invite trouble (Wilson & Kelling, 1982, p. 31). To the degree that schools in disrepair resemble untended property, and particularly should they evoke negative associations of failure or compulsion, they may be attractive targets for vandalism or other crimes. The combination of deferred maintenance and deliberate destruction contributes to an impression of neglect and anarchy. Wilson and Kelling found that in a public housing project in Boston, "the greatest fear was expressed by persons living in the buildings where disorderliness and incivility, not

> Tips for New Teachers: Getting the Resources You Want and Need
>
> You want computers, books, a field trip? When pursuing resources, try to align your wishes with someone else's best interests. Perhaps a business group wants to see more technology in your school or a historical society seeks to increase attendance at a museum. There may be a local employer willing to donate employee time for a tutoring project in exchange for free advertising in school publications or local newspapers. Watch for the administrator who has a passion for a particular project or the foundation with grant money for specific purposes. If you are observant and flexible, there may be resources available that would invigorate your teaching and engage your students.

crime, were the greatest" (Wilson & Kelling, 1982, p. 32). In other words, the mere perception that the situation was out of control caused people to feel uncomfortable and even afraid. For new teachers, this kind of environmental degradation highlights an unstable footing for their own authority.

However, there is a larger environment that affects the school culture. It is the community environment. Given its proximity to noisy industrial zoning, the neighborhood surrounding Paula's school may never have been particularly desirable, but it was certainly not in its prime. The paint was peeling off many of the houses, and the yards were unkempt. Throughout the day, men clustered around the beat-up cars that lined the streets. Paula explained that she lived in the same greater metropolitan area as her students, but she admitted that she "wouldn't feel safe" living in this neighborhood. Women may be especially attuned to the possibility of physical danger, and a deteriorating set of buildings in a neighborhood with loitering men can seem intimidating, particularly after school hours.

Educator Sara Lawrence Lightfoot claims that good schools are characterized by safety and order and that "this bedrock of authority provides an institutional coherence that is often expressed in teacher fearlessness" (Lightfoot, 1983, p. 346). In Paula's work environment, fearlessness seems not only unwarranted but also perhaps ill advised. The culture of this setting does not support it.

New teachers may learn to withdraw from a school environment they find indifferent or hostile. They may retreat into their own classrooms, frustrated or fearful or simply exasperated. This choice makes sense, conserving energy and allowing for concentration on teaching itself. Understandably, some teachers simply prefer helping students to haggling with adults. For new teachers, whose clout may be modest and whose skin may be thin, ignoring the broader school environment may look particularly appealing.

However, it can mean that they do not groom themselves for leadership opportunities, that they are easily manipulated by persuasive special interests, and that they are less effective in helping students understand and successfully negotiate the school's workings. To the degree that the environment is disorderly or baffling or contentious, the school culture may send new teachers walking briskly for the cover of classrooms of their own and, consequently, undermine their broader professional authority.

ASSIGNMENTS

One of the most far-reaching aspects of school culture is the distribution of teaching assignments, including grade level, subject matter, student population, classroom location, and schedule. There are structural constraints that inhibit rational planning. In California, for example, the state budget often is not determined until midsummer, so fiscally responsible administrators may postpone interviewing until they are authorized to make firm job offers. Meanwhile, springtime work includes sketching plans for the coming year, including tentative assignments for current faculty. For administrators, the course of least resistance is to grant the requests of current teachers whose immediacy and familiarity carry weight. Any leftovers may be cobbled together into an assignment for a teacher yet to be identified. By the time specific people are attached to each assignment, sketchy plans may seem fixed. Whether the assignments are reasonable or not, by the time the hiring process heats up in the late summer and particularly after the school year begins, teachers who have not yet signed contracts may be prepared to accept any job offer. Twice Paula had accepted job offers after the beginning of school, and she observed, "We [new teachers] get set up to fail" with ill-conceived teaching assignments.

New teachers may be particularly susceptible to onerous assignments. Young people tend to be more mobile than their older colleagues, and if they change jobs or move to a new place, they may find themselves caught multiple times in the snare of unreasonable assignments. Young women are perhaps particularly mobile as they relocate in order to preserve important relationships. Stephanie had moved to be near a boyfriend. Julie (Chapter 7) had moved twice with her husband, and she anticipated leaving her current school after her expected baby was born in hopes of finding a job closer to her home. Paula had resigned her job, effective at the conclusion of the school year, to join her fiancé in another city. Although it allows for a fresh start, this kind of mobility slows the process of gaining a voice in the creation of assignments. Unworkable teaching, schedule, or classroom assignments guarantee an induction of discouragement and deficiency.

Tips for New Teachers: Asking Good Questions

When interviewing or starting a new job, ask questions to convey your awareness of important issues and to highlight your strengths, concerns, and expectations. Here are a few questions to help assess school culture:

1. Philosophy: Is there a particular philosophy of teaching at this school? If the school is a magnet, charter, or private school, what is its particular mission?

2. Curricular Resources: What curricular resources are available to a teacher at this school (examples: science kits, textbooks, computers and software, garden plots, library facilities, art supplies)?

3. Linguistic Diversity: What languages are spoken by students at this school? What resources are available to help teachers communicate effectively with these students and their families (examples: bilingual aides, curricular materials, English language development programs)?

4. Discipline: What is the philosophy at this school about discipline? What is the protocol for dealing with an escalating discipline problem?

5. Parent Involvement: Is there a Parent-Teacher Association or other organizations to encourage parent involvement at this school? Are there regular parent-teacher conferences? Are there parent nights, school celebrations, or other special events for families?

6. Class Size: What is the average class size at the school this year? Which classes are largest/smallest and why?

7. Teacher Collaboration: Are teachers at this school collaborating on lesson planning, curriculum development, or other projects? What support is available for collaboration (examples: inservice or faculty meeting time, professional development credit, budget for new materials)?

8. Assignments: Is there a particular assignment for the teacher to be hired? What are the grade(s), subject(s), and schedule(s)? Is there an available classroom for the teacher to be hired? If not, what are the arrangements?

9. Tenure and Retention: What is the evaluation process for a new teacher? What are the requirements for tenure? How many teachers have more than ten years' experience? More than twenty?

10. Professional Development: What professional development opportunities are sponsored or supported by this school or district (examples: inservice, professional conferences, language or credential classes, partnerships)?

11. Union Relations: What are current issues for the union? Have teachers in this district ever held a strike? When and for how long?

12. Accreditation Review: During the school's most recent accreditation, what were the key findings, both strengths and weaknesses?

Teaching Assignments

Class assignments shape the culture of a teacher's work life. They may dictate a primary constituency such as students from a particular linguistic background or students with certain academic achievement levels. These characteristics do not exist in a vacuum but may be correlated with race, social class, or sex. In addition, a teacher's options in terms of curriculum and pedagogy are determined, in part, by her teaching assignment (Anyon, 1988). Perhaps most significant, teaching assignments may help determine the degree of professional satisfaction a teacher draws from her work. An appropriate, balanced assignment can yield great rewards, but a mismatch of talents, skills, or circumstances can be demoralizing.

At Paula's school, students were often grouped in classes that combined children from two or three grades. For example, the previous year Paula had taught Grades 4–6 together in one classroom. There was a significant range of academic and social maturity as well as "huge management issues," she recalled. There was simply "too big of a spread." Discipline problems are hardly surprising—given the difficulty of keeping all students engaged in appropriate curriculum—especially with a relatively inexperienced teacher. While new teachers may find preparing the curriculum for a single grade level challenging, attempting to grapple with two or three grade levels at a time is overwhelming.

The ongoing project of curriculum development is vastly complicated when the teacher works in a sheltered or bilingual class. In sheltered instruction, a teacher speaks in English but provides additional contextual support such as visual cues or simplified vocabulary to aid the comprehension of English language learners. In either situation, an effective teacher needs to present curriculum to different language populations. For truly bilingual teachers, that task may require extra preparation in translating handouts or materials. For the teacher of a sheltered class, the challenges may be multiplied. Students may speak a variety of languages with no common vocabulary. These classes may include children from all parts of the world with vastly different degrees of past formal schooling. In Paula's opinion, sheltered classes were much more difficult to teach than bilingual classes because of the greater differences in student needs, the obstacles to good communication, and the increased demands on the teacher. She observed, "People tell me that an experienced teacher couldn't do it any better, but why *aren't* they doing it?" It is a fair question. As a new teacher, Paula believed her chances of failure in these complex classroom situations were even higher than a veteran teacher's might be.

Although many teachers find working with recent immigrants particularly rewarding, the complexity of the task can be daunting, especially to inexperienced teachers. In urban areas where demand is great, new teachers, including young women, are quite likely to be assigned bilingual or sheltered instruction classes. They also are likely to be assigned any classes perceived by their colleagues as difficult or undesirable. These teaching assignments are crucial because they can subject new teachers to premature and unduly rigorous stresses. In this way, assignments determine, in part, a new teacher's effectiveness and professional satisfaction.

Schedule Assignments

Closely related to teaching assignments, schedules also shape a teacher's effectiveness and satisfaction. Some schedules are preferable to others, as Paula discovered. The history of her current job was revealing. Untenured, she had no firm job offer from her school the previous spring. During the early summer, the principal pieced together two half-time positions and offered the combined job to Paula, who accepted. As a result, she was responsible for some special projects and worked part-time as a release teacher. As a release teacher, Paula was a kind of in-house regular substitute, covering classes while the regular teachers worked on special projects. However, Paula explained, "I didn't want to be a sub," so she offered to do her own preparation instead of simply relying on the regular teachers' lesson plans.

Being a release teacher is not exactly parallel to being a regular classroom teacher. The person who is relieved, not the person who is relieving, has the status. Also, as a release teacher, Paula described less contact with both the students and their parents. In general, the parents wanted to communicate with the teacher who wrote the report cards. Since Paula's role called for supplements to other teachers' reports, parents often did not perceive her as an important player in their child's schooling. In addition, many of the parents of these students did not speak English, so Paula could not speak to them directly. Limited parent contact can erode a feeling of accountability among students for their behavior and academic performance.

The choppiest piece of this schedule for Paula was a multigrade class that met only thirty minutes a week for English Language Development. Given this clipped slot, there was little carryover from week to week. In Paula's case, the students came from a bilingual kindergarten as well as from English-only first and second grade classes. With rotating attendance, it was difficult even to learn the students' names. In a particularly unfortunate configuration, this brief morning class was sandwiched between two popular outdoor activities, recess and Physical Education. The class could only suffer by comparison, and it certainly suffered from the abrupt downshift in adrenaline. The students behaved badly. They were restless, and they fidgeted with books, pencils, and scissors as they sat on the carpet. Paula struggled, in another teacher's classroom with students she never got to know well, to impose order and present lessons.

On one occasion, she could not find any chalk. After fifteen minutes, a boy went to a cupboard and found some for her. Then she began writing stars and checks on the board to indicate good and bad behavior. The delay in giving this feedback, the dependence on the goodwill of a student, and the weeklong lag until their next session all undermined Paula. While carrying her own chalk would help, it would not address the larger limitations of this kind of schedule. Paula appeared powerless and at the mercy of the students, in part, because her schedule affords her little opportunity to appear otherwise. There is a perception of school life as relentlessly predictable, and it surely can be, but for someone in Paula's situation, every day is a startling adventure.

Schedules are one indicator of a teacher's authority. Veteran teachers generally can contrive workable arrangements. Workable schedules reinforce authority by allowing a teacher some familiarity with and control over the variables. Paula's schedule is chaotic and choppy. This kind of schedule indirectly undermines her by repeatedly putting her in positions where she is at the mercy of other people for resources, information, and reinforcement. New teachers are particularly likely to be assigned these kinds of convoluted schedules.

Classroom Assignments

At first, classroom assignments may seem trivial, perhaps more so than teaching or schedule assignments. After all, few schools have penthouses or picture windows to offer. At schools, the gradations are more subtle: slight size variances, proximity to the main office or other resource center, heat, and windows that open or at least do not face interesting distractions. In some settings, just having windows is a perquisite. However, a greater distinction than any of these is that between the teacher who is assigned a classroom of her own and the itinerant teacher.

Tips for New Teachers: Handy Supplies You'll Want

These items are not standard issue at many schools. Most cost money. If appropriate, you could ask if your school principal, department head, lead teacher, or Parent-Teacher Association has any funds that could help defray costs. Alternatively, you could publish a wish list and distribute it to parents toward the beginning of school. If you do, make sure to be explicit that parents are not obligated to donate anything.

Health and Safety

- Phone list of emergency numbers within and outside school (to post near phone)
- Band-Aids or a small first aid kit (to solve small problems and keep students with hangnails in the classroom)
- Plastic gloves (for blood)
- Diaper wipes or moist disposable towels (for spilled ink, drinks, or dirty hands)
- Instant antibacterial soap that requires no water (for rubbing on your hands when students sneeze on them)
- Tissue
- Cough drops or lozenges

Food and Drink

- Insulated mug or water bottle for hot or cold drinks (to keep your throat from getting parched)
- Granola bars, microwave popcorn, instant cocoa, herb tea, trail mix, raisins, crackers, or other nonperishable snacks (for hungry or distressed students or teachers)
- Napkins, paper towels, an extra mug, plastic spoons, dish soap
- Hard candies (if age-appropriate, to keep students quiet during a test or film or to reward them for good behavior)

Classroom Supplies

- Thrift store gloves, hats, or coats (for cold students)
- Old rags and cleaning solution (for dusting and cleaning desks)

Continued

- A lightweight stool (for sitting on while conferring with students at their desks)

- An anthology of suitable short stories or a basket of used age-appropriate books (for reading in the event of a lost lesson plan, broken VCR, or photocopier breakdown)

- Old magazines or catalogues (for art projects)

- Datebook or calendar (for tracking school commitments including faculty meetings, parent conferences, deadlines, and special events)

- Permanent marking pen (to write your name in big letters on all materials)

An aspiring teacher needs her own space to work. She will, of course, share this space with students. However, sharing with students and sharing with adults are quite different. In sharing with students, the teacher can be the boss, arranging the classroom according to her wishes and philosophy. In sharing with an adult, particularly during a temporary stint in another teacher's room, the young teacher is hardly an equal. Her presence is likely to be experienced by the other teacher as an encroachment and an inconvenience, and she is likely to have to work around another person's seating arrangement and wall displays. She is dependent on the classroom teacher's sense of fairness to get needed desk, drawer, and file space. She may not have a convenient or quiet place to work during her preparation time. For the same reasons new teachers may get stuck with undesirable teaching or schedule assignments, they may shoulder a disproportionate share of itinerant assignments, as well. Traveling undermines their fledgling classroom management skills, their ability to track papers, and their speed and accuracy in locating needed materials and supplies. Itinerant arrangements may make the development of authority unlikely for a new teacher by stressing existing points of vulnerability.

It is hard to overestimate the amount of additional stress that accompanies traveling for a new teacher. Traveling makes appearing organized and competent extremely difficult. Even a mundane matter such as starting class promptly becomes a feat of great magnitude. A traveling teacher often dashes in the door as the bell is about to ring and has to collect her thoughts, find her lesson materials, and present clear directives to the students before the opportunity passes. Her fluster sets the tone. Instructional time is wasted, and curriculum is constrained. It is difficult enough, for example, to lead a science experiment or art project in one's own room; it is easier to

---

Tips for New Teachers: Traveling Made Easier

If you are a traveling teacher, you have special logistical needs. Try the following:

- Ask for a locking cabinet, a desk, a bulletin board, and accessible drawer or counter space in each room, if possible.

- Consider getting a rolling cart or case to carry your materials.

- Use folders, boxes, carts, and bins that are brightly colored, clearly labeled, or otherwise distinctive. They will be easier to find and to identify as yours than standard issue office equipment.

- Create specific and accessible places for homework, lesson plans, and other papers, and use them. If you can avoid shoving papers indiscriminately into a bag or box in your rush to get to the next classroom, you can avoid the hassle of lost papers or time-consuming sorting at the end of the day.

---

skip these kinds of activities if they require hauling materials all around the school.

Traveling also takes a social toll. A traveling teacher is homeless at school, and that means she has no real neighbors. She is less visible, often less known, harder to find, and easier to ignore. On the other hand, she has more teachers with whom she is compelled to interact, although often in a subletting relationship. She is, in many cases, a guest in another teacher's room. She needs to ask permission and defer. Like many guests, her first priority may be ingratiating herself with the host. While ingratiating behavior may help her get along with her colleagues, it may actually hurt her chances of getting fair use out of the classroom.

Traveling makes it hard for a teacher to be in a position of strength when disputes arise. Her situation may compromise her ability to sit in judgment of others, as her job requires. An authoritative teacher is often one who gives students little raw material from which to concoct excuses, accusations, or shifted responsibility. She starts class on time so that she knows who is late, can point to missed material or disruption, and can move on. She collects homework, checks it in, bundles it securely, puts it in a safe location, and grades it together so that she can assert confidently that she is unlikely to have misplaced any. She does not lose momentum during a lesson by stopping to look for chalk. She has a default lesson plan, even if it is simply to return to an earlier activity or look ahead to a future one. If an activity sours, she is not bereft of resources. She has regular places and times where she is likely to be found, so that if a student needs extra help or

Tips for New Teachers: Managing the Paper Load

Assignments

- Determine how student papers or projects will be graded *while* you create the assignment so that directions correspond to evaluation criteria. Include this information on an assignment sheet, if appropriate.

- Create a grading sheet or rubric that students staple to the assignment before submitting. Be specific. Anticipate likely evaluative comments or suggestions and include them on the form. Circle the comments that apply. Include comments or a space for praise so you will be sure to give it.

- Photocopy cover or grading sheets on different colored paper to help keep assignments separate.

Grading Papers

- Collect work at the beginning of class. If possible, check in papers with a class roster in order to list missing assignments by the end of the class or the next day.

- If possible, grade at least a few papers on the day they are submitted in order to get momentum.

- Choose the most important errors to mark rather than marking everything.

General Administration

- Try to touch each paper, form, or memo only once. Read it, note important information, respond if necessary, and file or recycle it.

- During the school day, work in any tiny chunk of available time.

- Once you go home, work only in large blocks of time.

- Clear your desk every day before going home. Start fresh each morning.

a parent or colleague needs to speak with her, she is available. Without this kind of foundation, it is hard to be confident, and it is easy to be manipulated.

Perhaps the greatest toll of travel is the exponential increase in logistical details to track. The sheer number of variables makes organization improbable. Paula's recurring comments centered on these themes: "It's an impossible situation," "I'm thrilled with the idea of my own classroom—I've never had that luxury," and "I want to get more organized." Organization and work space are linked. It is difficult to be organized in someone else's space, and it may be inappropriate or futile to organize common space. It is certainly unwieldy and perhaps unwise for a teacher to carry everything she conceivably might need during a day's work. Paula's competence and confidence, two commodities sometimes scarce in new teachers, are significantly constrained by her classroom assignment. With increased odds of management difficulties, curricular limitations, logistical nuisances, and colleague negotiations, traveling new teachers may feel, appear, and perhaps be less competent than they might be in a classroom of their own.

Teaching assignments, schedule assignments, and classroom assignments are important components of school culture. They shape a new teacher's socialization to school life. Significantly, in the face of unnecessarily complex assignments and an unsupportive culture, Paula asked, "How can anybody feel good about herself doing this?" The phrasing of her question puts the burden of responsibility for her difficulties on herself. Some research suggests that girls, and perhaps the young women they become, are more likely than their male counterparts to attribute failure to insufficient ability rather than external constraints (Licht, 1987). While insufficient ability among new teachers is always a possibility, it is also likely that onerous assignments lead inexorably to these very difficulties and that their toll on young women will be magnified.

The school environment and the assignment process are important aspects of school culture. A third, though not final, piece of this culture is the quality and extent of relationships in the school context. Relationships are often central to the formation of identity and the foundation of confidence and authority.

ISOLATION AND CONNECTION

Isolation and connection are all about degree. Isolation is valuable and important in teaching. In appropriate doses, it allows a teacher to practice with curriculum and pedagogy, relatively free from interruption or premature evaluation. For new teachers in particular, this measured isolation can provide a needed buffer from outside interference and can foster confidence and competence. However, too much isolation can be lonely, stagnating, and unhealthy. Connection is important, too, for cultivating support networks, sharing resources, discovering and adapting others' successful ideas, and making friends. Given the culture of schools, with its emphasis on individuality, privacy, and autonomy (Clandinin & Connelly, 1995; Lortie, 1975), striking a balance between isolation and connection is difficult, perhaps especially for new teachers.

Tips for New Teachers: Making the Most of Difficult Circumstances

If you already have a difficult schedule, teaching assignment, or classroom environment, take action.

1. Identify the problem areas. What, in particular, is causing you trouble?

2. Ask for specific help without apology. Calmly explain that you need additional desks, fewer extracurricular duties, or simply advice.

3. Accept no additional assignments for the rest of the school year. Focus on your current responsibilities.

4. Experiment. Rearrange seats, try new curricula, change the morning routine, pair students differently, or call for parent volunteers. Alter existing negative patterns.

5. Get some fresh air. Ask to observe a colleague you respect or to attend a conference.

6. Lobby for changes for next semester or year.

A Difficult Balance

At times, Paula found that school life could be the worst possible combination: isolation from supportive relationships and unavoidable connection to obstructive people and processes. She recounted that when she worked at a previous school, she was hired to teach in a special program that was the subject of a political battle. During the ensuing debates about the program, an administrator warned her, "Don't talk in the staff room." Paula felt that this kind of guarded behavior was contrary to her nature. Like many new teachers, Paula was insecure about her teaching, a problem that too much isolation compounds. However, the potential benefit of teaching in a special program and having additional visitors and attention quickly degenerated into a political battle with complicated alliances, few of which seemed to include her. The admonition not to talk with colleagues made Paula feel very uneasy and cut off from potentially valuable sources of camaraderie, reinforcement, and support. The culture of isolation, mistrust, and hidden agendas was incompatible with her vision of herself and her work.

On the other hand, a culture that mandates complicated and inconvenient connections—however bureaucratically sound—makes isolation attractive. For example, Stephanie had to cancel a scheduled field trip because she had not followed the proper protocol thirty days in advance. There were people she viewed as extraneous who were supposed to be con-

> **Worth Discussing: Obstructive Colleagues**
>
> Although the school librarian oversees books, computers, and other resources for student use, she seems irritated by the chaos and disorder students inevitably bring into her work space. When you try to schedule your class for library visits, she creates obstacles and puts you off indefinitely. How should you respond?

sulted in her preparations. The purpose of this series of steps was unclear to Stephanie, but its practical function was to decrease the odds of field trips ever happening. As a side effect, Stephanie appeared disorganized, uninformed, and the subject of micromanagement. If her students were disappointed and angry at the last-minute cancellation, they had a logical target for their aggressions in the teacher who seemed unable to negotiate the school bureaucracy successfully.

A teacher cannot work entirely in isolation. At some point, she may need last year's standardized test scores, a videocassette player, assistance in testing a student for learning disabilities, petty cash reimbursement, or access to the principal. In fact, the more conscientious she is, the more likely she will need to work with a registrar, audio-visual clerk, resource teacher, school treasurer, or principal's secretary. Many of these roles will be filled by people who are harassed and busy, attending selectively to various requests. A teacher's ability to do her job effectively is contingent on getting needed services from these colleagues. Should they view her as bothersome, demanding, or in any way threatening, they have the power to subvert her by precluding her from doing her job or simply making her life unpleasant.

Clearly, the required investment of time and energy in negotiating these processes is significant, especially for new people who do not know the powerful gatekeepers or the shortcuts. Procurement of basic services should be the backdrop of professional life, but for new teachers, it easily may usurp center stage. One response to this problem is greater connection with colleagues.

Solidarity

There are voluntary and involuntary connections that come with being a member of any profession. For the young women teachers in this study, the teachers' union seemed to be both. When the union organized a strike over stalled contract negotiations, Paula, Helen, and Stephanie all supported the strike, although each expressed some ambivalence.

> **Worth Discussing: Taking a Stand**
>
> About half the teachers in your department or circuit support a pro-
> posal to eliminate ability grouping or tracking. They argue that this
> kind of grouping is discriminatory and harmful to students. About half
> the teachers oppose this proposal. They counter that some grouping
> allows for appropriate instructional levels for all students and rigor at
> every level. People on both sides are passionate and want your sup-
> port. You have mixed feelings about the issue, and you know that you
> will alienate colleagues no matter what position you take. What should
> you do?

In the tense weeks before the strike, Helen attended a teachers' meeting.
She described this confrontation:

> We had a meeting in my classroom, and we were talking about
> something. The woman next door was being, I thought, really nasty,
> and so I said . . . that she needed to lighten up and not be so belliger-
> ent, and she snapped back at me and told me to grow up and get
> over it. . . . I almost started to cry, and I got up and left my own class-
> room. And then I didn't speak to her for . . . months. And she is right
> next door.

Ironically, this effort at pre-strike solidarity is isolating and alienating.
The encounter is humiliating, as well. Helen's youth and inexperience are
highlighted in a mortifying way, and the resulting fissure becomes a land-
mark of that hallway. Even the inconvenience and awkwardness of not
speaking to her nearest coworker are not too great a price for Helen to pay
for dignity.

Nonetheless, Helen valued solidarity with her colleagues so much that
she participated in the strike. Absent strong philosophical alignment with
the union position, she had little incentive. As an untenured teacher, she
was especially vulnerable to being fired. She felt that the issues were mostly
holdovers from the time before she was hired. As well, she needed her salary. The entire staff supported the strike, and she felt that to be the only one
who did not would be very detrimental to her relationships at school. In the
end, she did not lose her job, and there were few lasting repercussions.
Nonetheless, solidarity—more social than philosophical—mattered enough
to Helen to be worth some risk.

For Stephanie, also, relationships were central to the strike story. Her
support for the strike rose not from her deep commitment to the union as an

---

Tips for New Teachers: Improving Your School Culture

Although one teacher cannot ultimately control her school's culture, she can influence it. School will be a warmer, more pleasant, more helpful place for new teachers if faculty and staff like each other and spend time together. The following ideas require some investment of time, but the potential payoff in improved school culture is great.

1. Find positive colleagues and eat lunch with them at least a few times a week.

2. Join or start a faculty/staff group around a common interest (books, writing, card-playing, Spanish conversation, etc.). One teacher organized a book recommendation list. He solicited brief reviews from colleagues and then distributed the results. The list generated community and enthusiasm for the world of ideas.

3. Join or organize a faculty/staff social club. Coordinate faculty meeting snacks, birthday recognition, potluck lunches, holiday celebrations, or commemoration of milestones such as births, weddings, and bereavements.

4. Cultivate a teaching partner, particularly if there are others teaching your same grade or subject.

5. Go out of your way to express sincere appreciation as often as possible. Note particularly administrative assistants, custodial staff, and support personnel.

---

institution but from her deep loyalty to her school friends who were union members. Stephanie considered not striking and explained her reasons for supporting the effort after all:

> I trust a lot of people at this school, and I know they feel the same way I do about things, and I know they've been through a lot more than I have. I felt like it would have been sort of disrespectful for me not to strike just because I was new and I didn't understand the issues entirely.

Stephanie's explanation is noteworthy, in part, because of its emphasis on her colleagues' judgment. She trusts them to act in her best interests as well as their own. Her desire to express solidarity with her colleagues far outstripped her conviction of the validity of the union's arguments.

CONCLUSION

In establishing professional identities, new teachers face two powerful and sometimes conflicting needs. They need connection, and they need isolation. In appropriate proportions, both connection and isolation lead to competence as well as confidence. For new teachers, this link may be particularly vital. To the degree that school culture makes connection and isolation incompatible, it particularly undermines the emerging authority of new teachers.

The experience of new teachers in schools is often frustrating on account of some widespread misconceptions they may have about school culture. If they imagine that schools will be helpful and supportive places because teaching is a service-oriented profession, they are likely to be disappointed. In the cases of Paula, Helen, and Stephanie, there is a shared sense that schools are surprisingly cold places. These new teachers find themselves on their own to figure out what they need to know in order to do their jobs. Worse, they may find that available resources and perquisites are distributed in ways that effectively penalize teachers for being new, inexperienced, and perhaps even agreeable.

Working in a school is not unlike climbing a great mountain, except that there is no summit and no glory. People may join functional groups, and ostensibly they have a common interest in staying together, pooling resources and expertise. However, in situations of duress—which may be most of the time, in some schools—sharing critical resources is costly enough that impulses of human compassion compete with the instinct toward self-preservation. It is the insidious and unanticipated competition that may be most surprising to new teachers, especially those who arrive fresh from college. They are part of the population being educated in schools. They are shaped, for better or worse, by the culture in which they come of age as professionals.

5 Beth

School Administration

My primary responsibility is to be a teacher of my kids [rather than] a staff member, and so I see my role is [to be] an advocate for them if they have a problem. Not that I am on their side, but it is just that it is my responsibility to be an advocate for them.

Beth

Beth clearly enjoys her job. In her four years of teaching, all at the same school, she has immersed herself in her work and has reaped tremendous rewards for herself and her students. Her unflagging energy and great affection for her students have helped her to impose a workable structure in a challenging environment characterized by transience and poverty. Beth is fluent in Spanish and well versed in Latino culture, and in a school with a burgeoning population of Spanish-speaking immigrants, she is well situated to establish herself as a valued and authoritative teacher. She commands respect and attention from students, parents, and colleagues. Given her interpretation of her professional role as an advocate for students, it is not surprising that Beth actively seeks engagement with the school administration. Almost from the beginning, she has sought out leadership opportunities for herself and prodded colleagues and administrators to do better. Beth's successes undoubtedly are linked with temperament, bilingual facility, and relentless work habits. However, it is her persistent dealings with the school administration that may ensure the widespread credibility she enjoys.

Beth entered teaching without benefit of a full-fledged teacher training program, instead opting to complete the Teach for America summer im-

Meet the Teacher: Beth

Age: 26

Education: B.A. Spanish

Professional Training: Teach for America, teaching credential

Number of Years Teaching: 4

Grade Level: Combined 5th–6th

Class Size: 30

Special Assignments: Multigrade class, looped class for three years

School Enrollment: 1,000

Schoolwide Eligibility for Subsidized Lunch: 90%

Schoolwide Student Ethnicity: 50% African American, 40% Asian, 10% Other

Schoolwide Achievement Scores Compared With National Average: Significantly below

mersion preparation. As a result, her initial investment in teaching, in terms of both time and money, was relatively small. However, Beth says, "Teaching energizes me," and she has found it rewarding and enjoyable. She reported that she had lots of experience with leadership in her earlier life, but when she started teaching, she felt that the stakes were suddenly higher. She worried about causing psychological or academic harm to students. As "the only person teaching them that year," she felt a burden of responsibility. She was not new to being in charge, but she was new to teaching and being the only one in charge of a very important enterprise that she had little experience in doing.

Admirably, Beth is finding her way. She requested and was granted the opportunity to teach the same class of students for three years. This situation allowed her to build rapport with students and parents over an extended period of time, at least by school standards. The results were obvious in her classroom. Unlike many other new teachers, she did not need or attempt to micromanage student behavior. Relying heavily on student self-direction, she was able to minimize the need to regulate behavior closely. She scripted complicated simultaneous activities, trained the students in their roles, and then trusted them to handle the responsibility. Her methods simplified classroom management and decreased the perception of nagging, but they required the firm grounding in expectations that was possible to develop over three years. As well, Beth actively included the Spanish-speaking students in her lessons. She patronized a neighborhood library dedicated to Spanish-language texts to check out books on the ancient civilizations that the students were studying. She created step-by-step assignment sheets in two languages. She traveled to Macchu Picchu in Peru over her spring break, she said, "Half for fun and half to take slides so I can teach about the Incas." She opened her classroom to students at recess and lunchtime for extra help with schoolwork, but she also stocked games and puzzles, and students congregated around her of their own choice. Her teaching duties largely under control, Beth was free to pay more heed to the school universe outside her immediate orbit, including the administration.

In general, as young people begin to assume leadership positions in the institutions that have shaped their lives—families, congregations, businesses, communities, and governments—they are confronted with the blemishes and structural flaws that are part of those institutions. While the flaws themselves may not be surprising, beginning to discern their complex, deep-rooted, and systemic origins may be a revelation for idealistic young people. Young teachers may be surprised to discover that making a big contribution is harder than they imagined from the comfort of the outside. Their ability to make a difference may be circumscribed by their meaningful participation in school administration. Given the limited authority of many new teachers in particular, this kind of participation may be intimidating, unrewarding, or simply unlikely. However, eventually every teacher has some encounter with school administration, often in the form of committee work, supervision and evaluation, and the principalship.

COMMITTEE WORK

One of the most logical and perhaps unavoidable ways for a young woman teacher to be involved in school administration is through committees. In Beth's school, every teacher is automatically part of a grade-level committee, but there is also appointed, elected, or voluntary service on committees formed to plan staff development, organize social events, recommend new textbooks, or select new office equipment. Some young women teachers, such as Stephanie and Paula, volunteer to serve on multiple committees as a way of getting to know other faculty members and having some say through the committee's collective voice. Ironically, Stephanie said that she found a voice through committees, although she admitted she did not say much. However, simply participating in committee work can help an individual teacher feel more effective in the larger school. It heightens her awareness of decision-making processes, makes her more visible to others, and helps her to understand the broader school context better. For some new teachers, the increased confidence, visibility, and voice may be well worth the investment in committee time.

Confidence, Visibility, and Voice

Beth found that serving on a schoolwide science committee "gave [her] an 'in' with the staff." At a time when science was receiving particular scrutiny, this committee generated significant interest and attention. Consequently, Beth found herself in the limelight as her committee assumed responsibility for monthly staff development workshops. This visibility brought heightened status. First, Beth had a chance to build a base of camaraderie in this subset of the whole faculty. Later, she developed confidence as she represented the committee in front of the whole faculty, sometimes leading inservice workshops. In this role, Beth could raise issues with the faculty as a member of a committee rather than as an individual with a gripe. She reported, "[The committee] gave me the opportunity and expertise" to pursue her leadership inklings.

In effect, serving on this committee gave Beth a visible group affiliation, a focus, and allies. It provided a kind of public identity. Though committee work can be alienating, alternately it may ease the damaging effects of teacher isolation and provide some reasonable expectation of support in contentious faculty discussions. It provides an excuse and a nonevaluative purpose for meeting with principals and other administrators. Significantly, a committee can bring a group of teachers together, often across the usual boundaries of grade level, classroom proximity, gender, or age, and it focuses their attention on a common goal. This concentrated time with a small group of colleagues may allow friendships and alliances to arise, providing a nonthreatening setting that some new teachers may find more comfortable than large group interactions. Committee work can provide desired opportunities to raise concerns as well as promote and implement responses. The belief that she was involved in organized efforts to make her school a better place sustained Beth through some periods of frustration.

Beth entered teaching with a sound visceral understanding of social dynamics, and committee work helped hone her instincts. She learned to observe carefully before entering any fray. Perhaps more important, Beth believed, "You need to steel yourself" in order to "learn to play the game." The transition from observer to active participant is hard for those who shy away from conflict, as women sometimes do (Tannen, 1994). In contrast, Beth "learned to ignore some criticism and say, 'So what?' if others disagree." When the inevitable conflicts arose, "Instead of getting hurt and sad, I got [angry]," she said. As a result, she held her ground instead of withdrawing. Her comfort with engaging in conflict and with crossing her colleagues, if necessary, set Beth apart from many of her new teacher peers. Committee work provided ample opportunity for both the development

---

Worth Discussing: Committee Service

You are asked to serve on a district committee by its chair, a district administrator. Although you barely can keep up with your own preparation and grading, you agree. At the first meetings, you notice that the teachers on the committee say very little. When you offer input, the chair listens politely and then proceeds as if you had said nothing. Silently, you begin to question the purpose of this committee and even to wonder if the purpose of each meeting is to generate minutes for the school board. What should you do?

---

and showcasing of Beth's professional identity. For new teachers, committee work can be a springboard out of obscurity, loneliness, and powerlessness.

Token Inclusion, Futile Exercises

Unfortunately, committee work is not always rewarding. It can be a distraction or a blather of endless debates. Sometimes the work of a committee appears to be fabricated. Teachers may be consulted in order to satisfy some external function only to have their recommendations ignored. Other committees may be chartered to solve a problem that either cannot be solved at all or else cannot be solved at the current level of information and support. This futile committee work can be irritating and agonizing, particularly for young women teachers who may seek or expect outcomes that are universally satisfactory.

For instance, Stephanie served on a textbook adoption committee charged with selecting new texts for teaching reading. She described the experience as "frustrating" and "political." There was a rumor circulating that schools could purchase either English Language Development materials for second language learners or Language Arts curriculum designed for native speakers, but not both. No one on the committee could positively confirm or deny the rumors, so the teachers felt that they did not have all the information they needed to make intelligent and informed recommendations. To complicate matters, Stephanie believed that there was pressure from state educators to select materials explicitly designed for standardized test score improvement in order to justify expensive statewide class size reduction. Most strikingly, however, Stephanie was not sure if a decision had been reached at the end of this day-long meeting. The outcome—along with the key constituencies, the rules, the agenda, and the constraints—was largely beyond her ken.

In this case, Stephanie attends a meeting because the district administrators believe that teacher input is important or at least politically expedi-

> Tips for New Teachers: Effective and Rewarding Committee Work
>
> - Choose carefully. If possible, join committees with useful functions that you care about. Limit the number to one or two.
>
> - Watch and listen. Develop an early understanding of the issues and interpersonal dynamics. Being attentive precludes doing unrelated work during meetings.
>
> - Participate. Any meeting worth attending is worth active participation. Speak, vote, or be cited in the minutes.
>
> - Keep it snappy. Use nonverbal cues to express some opinions: nod, frown, raise an eyebrow. It is unnecessary and time-consuming to repeat yourself or others.
>
> - Achieve closure. Ask, "What decisions do we need to make before leaving today?" or "What do we need to do before our next meeting?"

ent. She fills a spot but is not provided adequate information about the purpose and parameters of this committee. While the other teachers seem to share some of her confusion, for new teachers, district-level committees can be particularly frustrating because they come with more and unfamiliar layers of bureaucracy. New teachers are often not savvy or cynical enough to evade district commitments, but neither are they knowledgeable or influential enough to make participation on these committees more than symbolic.

For some new teachers, it may be that the value of this kind of committee work is not to accomplish the stated business but to educate themselves about the larger organization. Their initial participation may come in the form of attendance alone. Young women, who tend to be accommodating in accepting these service assignments (Martin, 1994) and who often strive to be consensus builders, may be particularly desirable candidates for these ultimately symbolic roles, at least until they accumulate enough experience to have stronger preferences and expectations. To the degree that district committee experience for new teachers is negative, they may learn to eschew broader interaction and understanding of educational politics, which may constrain their confidence outside their immediate classrooms and schools as well as their future career options and their professionalism.

Token participation in school-level committees can be alienating, too, as Helen discovered. She served briefly on her school's staff development committee. Expecting to help build the program, she was nettled to discover that the committee had a preexisting agenda that she was not sure she liked. She found determining an appropriate and comfortable degree of participation to be challenging:

> As a new teacher last year, I felt very awkward about being very opinionated because I kind of feel like, *I am brand new, what do I know?* I may think I have some ideas, but I need some more time to figure out whether they are really valid or not before I go around telling other people, *Well, I think we should do this.*

On a committee with a strong leader and existing direction, Helen felt superfluous. After three committee meetings, she stopped attending. While the symbolic participation was galling, Helen explained, "It was also a time issue. . . . I didn't feel like we were getting much accomplished." For Helen, busy with an onerous teaching assignment, being a token participant was insufficient inducement to merit her time.

Karen (Chapter 6) found that her role on one committee was less about tokenism than displacement. She recounted:

> I was sort of told that I was going to be on the Leadership Team, so [I should] sign up. And I said okay, and then I also heard people say, *Well, we really don't want So-and-So on the Leadership Team any more so we are going [to get] her on a different committee.* . . . They definitely smoothed my ego by saying, *We think you are a great writer, so we want you to do this,* and at the time I was probably like a little fish biting a worm, [saying] *Oh, you complimented me, I will do anything you ask.*

Karen was a willing if somewhat uninformed accomplice in this takeover organized to alter the existing philosophical or social chemistry of the committee. Interestingly, she recognizes the flattery used to entice her, and she readily acknowledges the primacy of her need for affirmation in this setting where little is forthcoming.

Committee work is a varied experience involving difficult choices about allocating time and priorities. Always, there are trade-offs. If new teachers participate in committee work, they often enhance their professional competence through opportunities to develop networks, to become visible and known, to interact with administrators, to have leadership opportunities, and to discover how things get done in their schools. Committee work, though, has its downsides. It may retard the growth of a new teacher's instructional competence by distracting her from teaching responsibilities, encroach on her time for a private life, produce few tangible results, obscure any individual contributions, or involve her in faculty intrigues. For some women, these choices may be particularly difficult as they juggle a heightened desire for connection with colleagues with demanding caregiving responsibilities at home (Hochschild, 1989). They may need to balance the advantages of small group interaction against the disregard and frustration of token participation. They may need to measure their desire to have input against a desire to make no enemies. They may have to weigh the demands of their own classroom teaching against the hope to make a difference in the wider school or district. The reality may be that there is no viable alternative to committee work for one who seeks to influence the school environment.

SUPERVISION AND EVALUATION

As with committee work, supervision and evaluation are facets of school administration that touch every new teacher. Understandably, many new teachers are anxious about their performance and eager for the specific feedback, including praise, that they need to improve. Women, in particular, may expect criticism and suggestions for improvement to be expressed tentatively and embedded in affirmation (Tannen, 1994). However, schools are not currently set up to facilitate regular, meaningful discussion about teaching performance. Formal observations, if they happen at all, tend to be cursory, and evaluations are most likely superficial and vaguely positive. Although it has its advantages, this arrangement can be puzzling and unnerving for a new teacher who wonders whether "satisfactory" signifies a compliment, a warning, or merely the absence of egregious misbehavior. Ironically, when there is criticism, it may not come in the form of official evaluations but in off-hand remarks, anonymous parent complaints, and rumors. When feedback is infrequent, any one comment can assume disproportionate importance, often generating frustration or defensiveness. For women, who may internalize criticism more than some men, and for new teachers, who are inevitably insecure and isolated, the erratic flow of feedback can evoke anger and cynicism.

Supervision and Evaluation of New Teachers

As a new teacher, Beth found that there was an "isolation and lack of people coming in to take a look and evaluate what [she was] doing." She wanted "nonthreatening help" and wished the principal, Ervin, would evaluate and observe. Evaluation and feedback "shouldn't stop at student teaching," according to Beth, and the "lack of accountability" for quality teaching disturbed her. "What if I start being a poor teacher? Will I know?" she wondered. She believed that providing this kind of feedback was "[the principal's] job, and he wasn't doing it."

According the Beth, during her first year, Ervin dropped by her class twice for about thirty seconds each time. Then he asked her to sign required evaluation forms that indicated that he had observed her class on specific dates, some of which were days off when neither Beth nor her students had been in school. His comments were always positive. Beth interpreted this form to be a complete fabrication and resented Ervin's request that she sign it in order to cover for his omission. Nevertheless, Beth admitted, "I'd rather have [Ervin's style] than someone breathing down my neck" with excessive monitoring. Ervin had distributed a memo with a schedule of evaluation visits, but Beth reported that he "never came," even after she reminded him to complete his observations. Later, she saw him in the office, and Beth recalled that he reminded her, "You still have to sign your evaluation." A tenured teacher now, Beth replied, "You still have to *do* your evaluation."

From Beth's perspective, a desired and valued opportunity for feedback was squandered by a principal too disorganized or careless or preoccupied to complete even the shallow evaluation required in schools. She found the positive evaluation particularly galling. While it may indicate Ervin's general confidence in Beth, it may also be an attempt to co-opt her into signing a misleading—if not falsified—document and guaranteeing her silence on the matter. Ironically, although he is her supervisor, Beth attempts to hold Ervin accountable instead of the converse. Beth finds this role reversal "frightening" because there is so much opportunity for abuse and incompetence to go unchecked, especially with new teachers who need lots of coaching and mentoring. This system of evaluation serves no one. It fails to weed out poor teachers who should not be rehired or given tenure. It fails to provide essential feedback for the newest teachers who need the most help. It fails to offer professional growth opportunities or challenges to more experienced teachers. This kind of nominal evaluation is a disaster, particularly for new teachers who need interaction and feedback in order to develop instructional competence.

Stephanie, also, felt slighted by her principal. "I never get any feedback from the principal," she said. "She came, like, two times to see me, and she said, 'Well, I was in your class a lot doing other things.' I had this really bad student that she always had to . . . drag out of class." It was clear in Stephanie's mind that the principal's evaluative visits should have been separate from disciplinary or other administrative visits. For Stephanie, it was a lost opportunity:

> I don't think I knew what I was doing at all at the beginning of last year, and [I] was just sort of lost and doing things that I had seen other people do . . . and it would have been so nice for somebody to sit down with me and say, "You know, Stephanie, what do you want to do this year, and how can I help you do that?"

Even a highly organized and conscientious principal might be hard pressed to deliver the kind of evaluative support that new teachers may desire. These teachers are typically making lots of mistakes and feeling insecure. The newest ones do not have job security. They want help. They want feedback. They want assurance. Consistently, evaluation is undervalued by their principals. While there is variation in the quality of observation, the results are strikingly similar: The principal glosses over the evaluation as a formality or nuisance or obligation, leaving the new teacher dissatisfied and confused. If she is persistent enough to look elsewhere to fill the gap between needed guidance and official evaluation, she may turn to mentor or inservice programs.

Mentor and Inservice Programs

Since the evaluation process is brief and fairly superficial, many schools provide some kind of supplemental mentor support for new teachers. Typically, a mentor is a classroom teacher designated to serve as a resource to a new teacher. Mentors have several advantages over principals in this role. They are current classroom teachers and likely to be tuned in to present curricular issues or organizational strategies. Perhaps more important, unlike principals, mentors are ideally not tainted in the eyes of the new teacher by evaluative responsibilities. Their job is to help, not to judge.

While there is no guarantee that the personal connection between a new teacher and her mentor will be a strong and positive one, a poorly administered program can preclude meaningful connections. In Paula's case, the mentor program was a district program, and new teachers sometimes found themselves assigned to a mentor at a different school site. Paula was assigned a mentor from another school even though there was a designated mentor at her own. This arrangement, no doubt devised to serve the convenience or equitable distribution of assignments at the district level, rendered the arrangement useless. A mentor teacher from another site can offer little specific advice or insight into school-level politics, does not know well the players the new teacher must deal with most directly, and is too far away to be available for spontaneous or informal conversations. For mentors to be useful, they must be proximate, familiar with the details of the school, and influential in securing help. Consequently, Paula complained that she "got nothing out of the mentor program." This good idea, intended to help new teachers, was not helpful to her. Worse, it consumed resources and gave the appearance of addressing an important need that, in fact, went unfulfilled.

Similarly, inservice programs are designed to foster ongoing learning, encouraging teachers to learn, grow, experiment, improve, and avoid stagnation and burnout. Ideally, inservice fills in some of the gaps that supervision and evaluation do not. Nevertheless, these teachers universally observed that existing inservice programs were poorly planned and had weak follow-up. For example, Helen felt that inservice meetings were a "complete waste of time." Beth noted that, regardless of experience or background, all teachers are compelled to attend the same workshops. She reported that she sat through the same training two or three times in five years. Veterans quickly become antagonistic or simply fail to attend. New teachers, who perhaps need the inservice most urgently, may suffer disproportionately when this expensive opportunity is squandered. They need meaningful professional interaction with their peers and could benefit from practical and philosophical discussions on teaching, yet these programs often fail them. To the degree that new teachers encounter more management problems or are more reluctant to call attention to themselves and ask for help, they need this structured support more than their colleagues and languish more from its absence.

Supervision and Evaluation by New Teachers

One facet of professional development that is frequently overlooked in both teacher education and inservice is the art of supervising adults. While most teachers get some exposure to philosophies and strategies for supervising and evaluating students, they easily can enter the field without giving much thought to supervising and evaluating adults. This oversight is not a harmless one. Instructional aides, in particular, are supervised by classroom teachers who direct and evaluate their work. In practice, however, the relationship between teacher and aide may be much less straightforward. Status differences around issues such as gender, formal education, languages spoken, age, years at that school, rapport with the students, and administrative support can complicate matters of supervision and evaluation, particularly for new teachers.

New teachers need allies in their schools. Allies provide support and reassurance, but they may also galvanize support and clear the path to needed resources. As well, new teachers need to work comfortably in their own classrooms, without challenge from the only other adult present. In the pursuit of these goals, teachers in this study banished aides from their classrooms, ignored aides who undermined them, and tolerated unprofessional conduct in aides. If the evaluation process of teachers is poor, the evaluation process of classroom and school support personnel may be even worse. New teachers who are dissatisfied with the performance of instructional aides must choose between overt criticism of their closest colleague or else tacit sanction of inappropriate behavior or mediocre performance.

Beth was fortunate in that this conflict never arose for her. She supervised an "awesome" instructional aide, Rosa, for four years. Rosa, an immigrant from Central America, had been a teacher in her native country, so she not only spoke Spanish fluently, she had teaching experience, as well. "The kids love her," Beth said. In her first year of teaching, Beth found it "weird" to supervise someone who had more experience, but she and Rosa devel-

Gender Dynamics: Adult Evaluations

According to researcher Paula England, "Very few female jobs involve supervision of other workers, especially male workers" (England, 1992, p. 14). Although this reality is changing, there is not a strong tradition or expectation of adult evaluation among women teachers. Teacher education programs and district orientations are unlikely to include specific preparation to guide new teachers through this process.

oped a "cooperative relationship" based on the "exchange of ideas." According to Beth, there was "no discomfort" in this relationship. Rosa's Spanish facility supplemented Beth's own proficiency, and as a result, introduced no threatening imbalance. Interestingly, Beth reported that evaluation of instructional aides was "nonexistent" at her school and that she had never been asked to complete an evaluation form for Rosa. Free from the obligation to evaluate, happily paired with an aide who brought clear supplemental skills to her classroom, Beth described great satisfaction in her partnership with Rosa.

Helen was not so lucky. By her account, she was assigned an aide, Jean, who actively undermined her. Jean was older than Helen, had children of her own, had years of work experience as an aide, and spoke Mandarin. As a young woman in her first full-time teaching job with a bilingual Cantonese class, Helen had lots of good reasons to be tentative in supervising Jean. Helen reported that she began by treating Jean as an equal and saying, "Let's do this together." However, this posture proved awkward because Helen was, in fact, supposed to direct Jean's work. When she did give direction, Jean seemed resentful and uncooperative, perhaps because their roles were poorly defined. Their relationship unraveled quickly as it became apparent that Helen was in charge of someone who would not defer to her judgment. Helen explained:

> So the clerical things that I asked [Jean] to do, she did every single one of them incorrectly, so it was never a help. I saw this as just a protest that she didn't want to be doing that kind of thing, and then in the classroom she was just openly contradictory. So I would ask her to mediate a dispute where I wanted her to speak in Chinese, and instead of mediating it, she would tell me that I had the facts wrong, even though I had seen [the incident] and she hadn't been in the room.

Helen said, "I finally got to the point where I had to say to her, 'This is not OK. I am the teacher here. You are not the teacher.'" Understandably, this

> ### Tips for New Teachers: Supervising Adults
>
> Setting clear and appropriate expectations can ease the discomfort that evaluating adults sometimes creates. Ongoing and regular conversations can preclude misunderstanding. A candid conversation as early as possible about the following subjects can help.
>
> - What is the person's job description? What functions is she or he required or expected to do? What roles is she or he not allowed or expected to do?
>
> - What help does the teacher need most (examples: grading, clerical support, tutoring, management assistance)?
>
> - What particular skills, experience, or strengths does this person bring to the job? What does he or she enjoy most about the job?
>
> - What does the formal evaluation entail and when will it occur?

confrontation was unpleasant for both, and quickly the relationship became completely unworkable. Jean was reassigned, and Helen finished the year without the benefit of an instructional aide. She concluded from this experience:

> I would never handle another aide in the same way from the very beginning. . . . If someone is hired as an aide then I need to direct them more than I directed this woman, as a favor to them also, not to just leave [their role] wide open.

The very presence of an instructional aide violates the norm of classroom privacy. New teachers, like all teachers, need time alone with their students. Yet here is this aide, often older, often more senior at the school, often with children of her own, even children older than the new teacher, who is technically a subordinate. New teachers may reach out to this person as an ally simply to find that there can be only one boss. These teachers have enough challenges already without the addition of an adult who is anything but an asset. There is a cost, often hidden to new teachers, of working with an aide. Ostensibly, instructional aides decrease the ratio of students to adults, thereby improving the classroom climate and making instruction more effective. In fact, in some cases, aides create work for teachers. They require direction, planning, coordination, the maintenance of a relationship, and at least theoretically, evaluation.

Supervision and evaluation are important, and typically, they are slighted. New teachers often need and want support, but it is not usually a realized priority of the school administration. This observation is not necessarily an indictment of administrators. Rather, it is an observation of a system that places one person, the principal, in charge of many, many important responsibilities. In general, principals are stretched far too thin, and even the most conscientious are doomed to negligence of one duty or another. For many principals, evaluation of teachers simply does not merit the attention that disciplinary matters, public relations, test scores, or other administrative duties consume. That is not to say that principals do not care about the quality of their teachers. However, a wise principal learns to discern which duties are visible and which problems tractable, and teacher evaluation may be neither. For new teachers, the principal's role can be both perplexing and frustrating.

PRINCIPALS

Workers everywhere complain about the boss, and principals are not exempt from being easy targets for exasperated employees. While disgruntled teachers may emphasize the differences in their roles, in reality, principals face many of the same difficulties that teachers do. There are too many demands, insufficient training, conflicting constituency groups, and more responsibility than authority. Furthermore, principals do not have the security of tenure or the freedom from public scrutiny that many teachers enjoy. School administration can be difficult and thankless work. That said, the young women teachers in this study generally viewed their principals as poor leaders. Stephanie resented the way her principal preempted—with little notice—planned staff development time. Helen believed that her principal relied on her inappropriately to assure compliance with bilingual education regulations. Paula liked her principal but repeatedly mentioned that she had little time to help new teachers. Beth described her principal as "do-nothing," an administrator content to let any issues that were important, controversial, complicated, or time-consuming play out without his needed involvement. Karen (Chapter 6) believed her principal guilty of favoritism, cutting lots of slack for her closest friends on the staff and little for others. Only Julie (Chapter 7) had unqualified praise and support for her principal, and her unusual circumstances probably influenced her views.

These new teachers probably do not fully apprehend their principals' situations or perspectives. Nonetheless, the image remains that most of the principals are weak leaders who do not understand teachers' work or needs, renege on their obligations to teachers, and fail to support them or protect them from flak. This perception, accurate or not, has ramifications for new teachers. It means that they may be unlikely to seek guidance or resources from administrators, viewing them instead as evaluators or bureaucrats to be held at bay as much as possible. This decision cuts off new

Tips for New Teachers: Working Effectively With Principals

1. Read memos; be attentive during faculty meetings.

2. When problems arise, try other solutions and resources before involving the principal.

3. When you need the principal's involvement, be specific and concise about the issues, your needs, and the other solutions you have attempted.

4. Listen to evaluative feedback carefully. Try to make use of suggestions for improvement. If, after reflection, you disagree with an evaluation, explain your reservations clearly, using specific examples.

5. If the principal is distant, preoccupied, or unhelpful, try to cultivate another administrative mentor.

6. Make the principal look good. Whenever possible, speak highly of her to parents, support her priorities, and commend her successes. She will notice.

7. Promote trust and goodwill in your principal. Although your job can be done without his support and involvement, it often can be done more effectively and efficiently with them.

teachers from the person who may be the only one to make firsthand observations of their work, and, as a result, from the hope of helpful input. In addition, this disconnection from the administration makes the isolation of teaching even more profound. As a practical matter, no one is in the office to help. New teachers must work out their problems on their own, preferably without disturbing anyone elsewhere in the school. For young women, who may have more management problems than other teachers (Tannen, 1994), who rely heavily on external validation of their work (Belenky, Clinchy, Goldberger, & Tarule, 1986), and who languish in excessive isolation (Lortie, 1975), this arrangement can be particularly damaging.

The significance for new teachers may hinge on some confusion about the nature of school administration. The study teachers tended to assume that virtually all their difficulties could be solved by a competent and attentive principal, and consequently, they felt some resentment and anger as the problems persisted, assuming that the principal was not doing a good job. However, they may have attributed more power to principals than is appropriate. In fact, they may have lumped indiscriminately two very different sets of problems: those with origins in the school and those with origins in the broader society. Ostensibly, the in-school problems—including unbalanced assignments, lax discipline policies, inadequate evaluation, ineffective inservice, and unfair allocation of resources—might be eradicated by strong management. The broader problems, including uncertain school funding, insufficient health and child care, violence, poverty, sexism, and racism, among others, are not discrete problems as much as ongoing issues, and they are not within the control of a principal to address in any comprehensive manner. However, new teachers may look to the principal for relief from any of these problems with greater urgency and expectation than some of their colleagues. In many cases, they are destined to be disappointed.

Management

Sound management, the immediate stewardship of principals, is crucial to new teachers' authority. Effective management establishes priorities and procedures that help allocate attention and resources appropriately. Ineffective management, often characterized by impulsive lurching from crisis to crisis, rewards urgency over other kinds of importance. This approach to management means that new teachers are unlikely to get attention and support until they are in a critical condition. It undermines the focus and freedom from worry that are essential for instructional competence. Crisis management often means that essential activities are neglected and supposed routines are not predictable. In particular, the study teachers expressed frustration with the communication at their schools and with the habitual interruptions of their classes.

Communication

One of the early challenges new teachers face is learning to interpret jargon. As with many other professions, education is full of symbolic speech. For inexperienced teachers, this speech is easily confused with direct communication. Designed to elicit from its audience a sense of confidence and authenticity, this kind of communication is less about conveying information than impressions. For that reason, the information is easily garbled.

In spite of the ubiquitous public address systems, school communication is surprisingly difficult. Schools are not typically designed to facilitate easy or direct communication. Teachers work in separate rooms, some quite remote from the central office, and communication often happens slowly, haphazardly, and inconsistently through paper memos left in teachers' boxes. Among adults, there is little interaction during the school day, so communication is often hampered by infrequent opportunity. Then there is the matter of interpretation. Words do not carry the same meanings for all people, and school administrators who need to convey information often have to walk a fine line between adhering to expectations about vocabulary, content, and tone while attempting to filter the needed messages to the right people. Toward that end, some messages are deliberately coded for those who have ears to hear. However, ears to hear are usually trained ears, and new teachers rarely have developed them yet.

For example, in Beth's first year of teaching, she was assigned to the school's Leadership Team. One of this committee's first tasks was preparing for a Program Quality Review (PQR), an outside evaluation of the school's programs. Beth understood this assignment literally, as an opportunity for the school to conduct a self-study and get valuable feedback from outside observers. Her principal, Ervin, apparently took a less sanguine view of this process. He wrote the required documents himself and listed the Leadership Team members as coauthors. Since Beth knew nothing about this report, it upset her when her name appeared on it. She viewed this "ghost participation" as a fraud and a sham. When Ervin assigned her to this committee, he did not make it clear that her role was largely symbolic. When a new vice-principal was transferred to the school a year later, Beth was delighted to find an administrator who went "by the book" and truly wanted teacher involvement and input, as opposed to their mere appearance.

It is noteworthy that "by the book" is a virtue for Beth, as it is often a euphemism for unnecessary literalism. However, literal interpretation of instructions and guidelines is not an inconvenience or a threat to her. In fact, it is refreshingly comprehensible. Further, it reinforces her desire to provide input and have a voice. When Ervin usurps this role, he may imagine that he can represent teachers or streamline the process or even protect himself. However, Beth does not share this understanding. She resents being cut out. While the tangle of school policies and regulations is undoubtedly oppressive to principals, disregarding them in favor of efficient or unilateral action may penalize, exclude, or render invisible people who do not fare well in a free-for-all environment, including many new teachers.

In short, the goal of school communication is not always simple. Sometimes it is more about fulfilling an expectation than about providing clear, complete, unbiased information. Implied understandings, hidden agendas, and slippery definitions make it hard for new teachers to understand what is being said. Ensuing difficulties, sharpened by surprise, can lead new teachers to the conclusion that the administration communicates ineffectively. Right or wrong, that perception is a management problem.

Interruptions

A second facet of management that aggravates many new teachers is the problem of interruptions. In order to be effective, teachers need time that they can experiment with, shape, and control. Classroom life is filled with inevitable disruptions that can undermine a teacher: student quarrels, unusual weather, scraped knees, or an outburst related to troubles at home. To the degree that the school administration works to minimize these untimely breaks, it supports a new teacher in her work. However, when administrators allow last-minute schedule changes or unessential announcements over the public address system during class time, those colleagues become accomplices to the most unruly students thwarting the teacher's efforts. These interruptions undermine a teacher's authority by surprising her, rendering her previous planning ineffective. Interruptions demonstrate to the students that their teacher is not someone who needs to be consulted in important matters like scheduling. Disrespect of this kind implies that classroom instruction, the teacher's primary responsibility, is relatively unimportant. While interruptions do not affect only new teachers, their impact on those teachers may be particularly harmful. New teachers have less experience in guiding the class back to the lesson gracefully, fewer back-up lesson plans and ideas, and less status in refusing to heed interruptions, when possible.

Beth understood so thoroughly the need for freedom from interruption that she taught with her classroom door locked from the inside. Anyone who wanted to enter her room would have to knock, which is its own disturbance but allowed her to determine how quickly to open the door and whether or not to grant entrance. Nonetheless, Beth could not block out the in-house phone. On one occasion, she painstakingly prepared a science lab involving lots of materials. She arrived early, prepared each student table with the necessary supplies, and outlined the experiment on the board. At 8:55 a.m., just as the students had begun to conduct the experiment, the phone rang. After hanging up, Beth turned to the class and announced a "surprise change in schedule." The students were to report immediately to the gym for a dance assembly featuring students from the school. Beth proceeded to apologize for the schedule change and directed the students to leave their science materials out until after the assembly. The students cheered, taking a perverse pleasure in seeing their teacher's carefully prepared lesson interrupted. They returned from the assembly full of rhythm and motion, clearly charged up by the performance. Beth encouraged them to resume the experiment, but there was not very much time remaining before recess. Students who did try to go ahead were again interrupted when the recess bell rang, and students who procrastinated then returned from recess needing to start at the beginning.

This interruption devastated the morning lesson. Instead of focused science exploration, the class was characterized by lost momentum, repeated instructions, wasted time, and an epidemic of student fingers drumming on desks all leading toward the culmination of recess. Moreover, Beth's careful work was sabotaged for an assembly featuring students from the school. They are not out-of-town celebrities whose unannounced visit came as a welcome but unanticipated surprise. There is no reason, other than poor planning or communication, for this kind of assembly to be unexpected. Even so, Beth apologizes to the students without a whiff of sarcasm.

Karen (Chapter 6) faced a related dilemma. She took her class to an optional Earth Day assembly, after which they returned to class. As they began a vocabulary lesson, an announcement came over the public address system inviting all interested classes to a repeat performance to begin in two minutes. Although Karen's students clamored to go, she told them that they would not attend the second performance. In this case, Karen is put in an awkward position by a last-minute public invitation. The announcement galvanizes the students to begin lobbying the teacher. As a result, Karen may come across as a killjoy who is too fixated on vocabulary to take time out for a schoolwide celebration. This depiction is unfair, inaccurate, and inevitable under these circumstances. Karen did take her students to the first assembly. She planned ahead and made a reasonable and responsible lesson plan. Given this kind of interruption, planning was her first mistake.

Surprise assemblies, like many other interruptions in the teaching day, are to a significant degree controlled by the administration. In a school where administrators protect teaching time, assemblies and other atypical arrangements would be planned in advance, allowing teachers to develop schedules around them or perhaps choose not to attend them. The premise would be that teaching is central, and other, auxiliary activities are encouraged only insofar as they do not interfere with it. Similarly, the use of the public address system, in-house phone calls, student or adult messengers bearing nonurgent information, school maintenance crews, or any other intrusion on class time is an interruption. While principals cannot control the actions of every student or adult on campus, they can make clear policies protecting teaching time and consistently honor these guidelines. Principals who are good managers do not allow interruptions that penalize teachers who are prepared.

Accountability

Another important function of principals is establishing accountability. Accountability is vital to a productive working environment. It helps people get credit for their good work, and it calls attention to areas that need improvement. Generally, while some people are hurt by accountability, the overall environment is enhanced by it. Schools, given their compartmentalized nature, are tough places to bring accountability to bear. It is difficult to know just what people are doing in their individual classrooms. While that news may be favorable for any slackers, it is in many ways unfortunate for new people who need attention, training, and feedback. For new teachers, accountability is particularly important in promoting competence. If they have weak skills, a system of accountability makes discovery and amendment more likely and reduces the odds that they will lead quiet lives of

> **Worth Discussing: Administrative Support**
>
> One of your students is chronically disruptive during class. After numerous attempts to improve the situation, you schedule a parent conference and invite an administrator familiar with the situation to attend. At the conference, the parent becomes defensive. The administrator mentions that you are a young and inexperienced teacher and implies that your classroom management skills are weak. The parent leaves with an air of vindication. Certain that the situation is only going to get worse, you feel belittled and abandoned by the administrator. What should you do?

instructional desperation. Conversely, if they are outstanding teachers, the absence of a system of accountability hides their successes and fails to reward their pedagogical growth. When lax accountability fosters a climate where mediocrity and incompetence are tolerated, new people have reason to feel discouraged about their prospects of developing competence.

Beth, for example, expressed frustration with the process of accountability in her school. When she began teaching, there was a vice-principal at her school who, in her judgment, was "lazy" and "didn't do his job." He was in charge of planning inservice activities, but according to Beth, he did not prepare, so the time was often wasted. Beth reported that he interrupted her class and spoke condescendingly to students. Eventually, even though she was a first-year teacher, Beth became so indignant that on three occasions she asked him to leave her classroom. In addition, according to Beth, there were allegations surrounding him of harassment of parents and other staff members as well as of embezzlement. Beth and other teachers wrote up their complaints about this vice-principal. Beth recalled, "We were sure we were going to get rid of him," and she was bitter when it appeared they would not. Beth believed that it was typical of her district to do nothing in spite of evidence of wrongdoing she found convincing. Previously a principal, this man had been demoted to vice-principal, and he quit as he was about to be reassigned as a classroom teacher.

While it is difficult to know exactly what the vice-principal did in this case, it is clear that eventually he was forced out of his job. However, it took years. Delayed too long, accountability grows tepid. Beth was wary of the vice-principal from the beginning of her employment at the school, and she found the grinding process of district accountability unacceptably slow. Her mettle in asking him to leave her classroom is evidence of her own desperation and sense of obligation as a student advocate. Part of Beth's disgust with this situation lies also with Ervin. As principal, he worked more closely with the vice-principal than anyone. Their offices were adjacent, and they attended the same meetings. If Ervin did not know that there were problems, he should have. In fairness to him, it may be that he had to let the wheels of due process roll forward at their own pace, or he may have felt a personal connection with his colleague that made intervention difficult. However, Beth's impression, right or wrong, is that Ervin knew about whatever problems there were and did nothing. As a conscientious employee, she is demoralized to see a coworker, especially an administrator, contribute little and detract from the school enterprise.

Beth is bothered by the detractors, but if she is a little wistful for greater accountability, it may be that she is also concerned about the people like herself she calls "do-gooders" who stay late, take on unremunerated assignments, and seem to work tirelessly helping students. Lax accountability cuts both ways. While Beth has made peace with the current arrangement, as good teachers often must, it is a little dissatisfying.

Given their frequent desire for feedback and support, as well as the idealism that often accompanies their visions of teaching, new teachers may be particularly bothered by this arrangement. They may place a fair amount of the blame on their principals. New teachers attribute blame appropriately when they see principals tolerate unprofessional behavior, shrink from unpalatable disciplinary responsibilities, and neglect their evaluative or mentoring duties to teachers. However, on other occasions, new teachers attribute blame inappropriately, or at least too confidently. They sometimes assume that motivated and informed principals could fix problems immediately. Certainly, principals can make a difference; however, they face real constraints. They often have the unenviable task of allocating insufficient means. They are subject to the supervision of the school board and superintendent, and they are hemmed in by the education code, union legislation, and tradition. They make changes at their peril, potentially alienating influential veteran teachers who have a stake in the existing configuration. They are also busy with their traditional duties of documentation, personnel management, parent meetings, student discipline, and financial matters, increasingly augmented with fund-raising and public relations obligations. While negligence and malfeasance are unflattering in any light, it may be that, over time, some of the principals the young women teachers in this study look upon with disdain will begin to seem able or at least tenacious.

CONCLUSION

The principal is a powerful figure in a school and has the ability to make the induction of new teachers smoother and more successful through skillful management and appropriate accountability. For new teachers, strong management can promote clear and effective communication and freedom from interruption that make instructional competence possible. Accountability creates an environment where teachers can expect regular supervision and feedback, as well as appropriate recognition.

To the degree that new teachers choose their vocation in order to help students, they may not anticipate the importance that school administration will play in their professional lives. In fact, even in a loosely centralized organization like a school, administration touches every aspect of teaching life: It encompasses how decisions are made, which policies are adopted and how they are implemented, and the ways assignments are formed and resources allocated. Committees, with their potential for heated debate or quiet reflection, are often the venues of school administration. For new teachers, overwhelmed with the demands of preparation and grading, prioritizing assignments and opportunities may necessitate particularly difficult choices. Supervision and evaluation may be surprisingly uncomfortable for new teachers, as well. When these teachers are the subjects of evaluation, they may find that the standard format fails to address their desire for ongoing feedback in a supportive context. When they supervise others, they may be caught off guard by the difficulty of evaluating close associates. Finally, in their interactions with principals, new teachers may find that their expectations for management and accountability, realistic or not, are disappointed. Developing professional competence requires moving beyond perplexing and aggravating incidents toward a productive working relationship with the school administration.

6

Karen

Professional Judgment

[At first] I wanted to take on everything but was incapable. Now I've scaled down my scope and by doing so, I've been able, ironically enough, to be more effective.

Karen

After graduating from a prestigious university, Karen traveled, wrote a novel, and worked as a salesclerk at Macy's department store. Then she decided to try teaching and enrolled in the summer immersion training offered through Teach for America. Karen is originally from the San Francisco Bay Area suburbs, and coincidentally, her initial placement brought her to this district in her native region. Karen found teaching stressful. She said, "In September, the shot goes off, and I'm in the race. I come up for air on the weekends." In fact, she reported, she does not sleep well during the school year and wears a mouthpiece to prevent her from grinding her teeth at night. She tried not to bring any work home at night, although she believed she would be less distracted in the classroom if she did. She said, "We [teachers] get a lot of our self-worth from doing a lot." Karen does do a lot, although, as she indicated, she was trying to make more deliberate choices to increase the effectiveness of her efforts. Instead of working furiously in multiple directions at once, she was learning to evaluate and choose where to expend her energy. In short, she was developing some professional judgment.

Professional judgment attempts to reconcile two conflicting ideas: (a) the practical need to act in a timely and justifiable manner, and (b) the need to reason and deliberate carefully over complex matters. Whether responding to a student dispute, explaining curriculum choices to parents, justifying a grade, assigning penalties for infractions, or attempting to motivate a

Meet the Teacher: Karen

Age: 27

Education: B.A. English

Professional Training: Teach for America, teaching credential

Number of Years Teaching: 5

Grade Level: Combined 3rd–4th

Class Size: 28

Special Assignments: Multigrade classes, sheltered instruction

School Enrollment: 600

Schoolwide Eligibility for Subsidized Lunch: 75%

Schoolwide Student Ethnicity: 75% African American, 15% Latino, 10% Other

Schoolwide Achievement Scores Compared With National Average: Significantly below

student, a teacher's professional judgment is invoked. Some decisions allow the luxury of unhurried deliberation, but others require an immediate and unambiguous decision, often with imperfect or incomplete information. Ultimately, professional judgment is more about making defensible choices than arriving at the definitive ideal.

In general, these new teachers felt keenly the moral ambiguity of many curricular choices, discipline strategies, and school policies. The teachers' awareness of these issues sometimes made it difficult for them to make judgments unequivocally. Consequently, at times they appeared tentative and vulnerable. To the degree that they balk, vacillate, or hedge, new teachers may undermine their own credibility. Inexperienced persons often appear to be weak as they weigh options. Further, in an effort to make reparations for past compromises or mistakes, they may make contradictory and inconsistent choices. Sound judgment implies pattern. This chapter examines Karen's patterns in addressing practical dilemmas with moral overtones.

MORAL DILEMMAS IN TEACHING

Teaching is full of wrenching trade-offs, fragile compromises, and quandaries where principled responses are difficult to formulate and implement.

> ### Gender Dynamics: Careful Deliberation, but Timely Action
>
> To the degree that their emphasis tends to be on individual relation-ships, some women may be particularly prone to decision paralysis when confronted with an onslaught of complicated choices affecting the lives of others. The call to honor individual relationships may impede timely judgments by making efficient but flawed categories and generalizations unacceptable. As well, in honoring relationships, women may be particularly reluctant to disappoint or offend, and consequently, loath to make judgments that require the sacrifice of their own or someone else's prized value. The attention to the idio-syncrasies of individual relationships that is characteristic of some women is a valuable tool for grasping the nuances of different situa-tions, but that very strength may encumber the rendering of swift and unapologetic judgments when needed.
>
> Teachers who are reluctant to render judgment leave open issues that should be resolved and forgotten, or at least made peripheral. Worse, delayed deliberation can undermine the connection between events that is critical for students to understand. To be meaningful, repara-tions must swiftly follow their offenses, and mistakes must be cor-rected while they are still relevant. Failure to attend quickly to these matters conveys a sense of carelessness about the moral environment that is a poor practice for teachers (Sockett, 1993).

Regardless of the announced course of study, the curriculum is always, in part, about learning to function in a shared world. It is about developing an appreciation for ideas, aesthetics, and abilities. More than anything else, however, it is about people. Feminist educator Nel Noddings argued:

> Among the intangibles that I would have my students carry away is the feeling that the subject we have struggled with is both fascinat-ing and boring, significant and silly, fraught with meaning and non-sense, challenging and tedious, and that whatever attitude we take toward it, it will not diminish our regard for each other. The student is infinitely more important than the subject. (1984, p. 20)

The student *is* infinitely more important than the subject. However, as these new teachers discovered, honoring the centrality of students in school is not easy. Students have competing needs, and in some cases, their needs cannot be honored simultaneously, if at all.

Tips for New Teachers: Reflective Living in Schools

In a reflective life, thinking about important moral and ethical dilemmas is an ongoing process, punctuated by moments of decision and action. However, for new teachers, a more likely description may be days of rapid-fire action, punctuated, for the lucky, by moments of reflection.

To help you keep your focus on important as well as urgent matters, try writing down a few of your most basic beliefs about teaching. Then write down the rules, policies, and consequences you want to establish in your classes. Are the two lists complementary? If not, revise them. Post them next to each other in a place where you and others can see them often. Here is an example:

Principle #1: Instructional time is inviolable. My goal is to involve every student every day in meaningful interactions with a rigorous curriculum.

Policy #1: Class begins promptly when the bell rings. Students must be in their seats with pencils, paper, and other class materials ready. The agenda, announcements, and assignments will be written on the side chalkboard.

Principle #2: Students want and need a well-organized, orderly class.

Policy #2: Anyone who interrupts or interferes with instructional time must stop immediately or face consequences. If a problem arises, I will caution the student about the unacceptable behavior. If the problem persists, I will take as many of the following steps as necessary to resolve it: move the student's seat, remove the student from the classroom temporarily, call the parent, or schedule a meeting with an administrator.

Principle #3: Students and parents deserve to know exactly what the expectations and standards are.

Policy #3: An overview of the year's curriculum and class policies will be available to students and parents at the beginning of the year. A more specific calendar will be distributed at the beginning of each month. Typically, assignments will be handed out on Mondays and due on Thursdays. Grading criteria will be included on each assignment. Report cards will be issued four times a year. Parent conferences will be held once a year. Parents may request conferences at any other time, as well.

Determining the best interests of individuals and classes, selecting methods and content, and allocating resources create difficult dilemmas that are confounded by the diverse racial, ethnic, and class backgrounds of the students. The need for professional judgment in attempting to create a moral ethos in classroom teaching is pervasive. For those who choose teaching in order to work with children and make a difference in the world, a moral core of teaching may be particularly vital. Karen's struggles for fairness, integrity, and an appropriate jurisdiction left her vaguely dissatisfied.

Fairness

Although its definition and application may be contested ground, fairness is indisputably part of teaching. As Hugh Sockett noted, "Fairness is central to teaching in one particular respect. Teachers are the first adults most children meet who are in positions of authority but are unrelated to their personal family lives. Teachers represent adult life" (1993, p. 82). However, as new teachers discover, fairness is often a matter of perspective. Weighing the needs and wishes of individual students, the class, colleagues, administrators, parents, and herself can be overwhelming for a new teacher. Since it is sometimes impossible and often unwise to regard all demands equally, a teacher must prioritize her commitments.

Karen learned first-hand about the discomfort of these kinds of judgments when she ran afoul of the school psychologist, Dr. Hampton, over a boy named William. A student with special needs, William had a long history of academic and behavioral difficulties, but in the weeks preceding this confrontation, his attitude had deteriorated, according to Karen. During a class meeting, he had interrupted and ridiculed several classmates. The previous week at recess, he had dragged a girl down a hill on the school yard, causing a gash from her waist to her ribs. After a one-day suspension, he tried to drag another student down the same hill. Karen had changed his seat, called home, referred him to the administration, and consulted with Dr. Hampton, who met weekly with William. Nonetheless, in spite of Karen's efforts, she believed that the situation was degenerating.

On this occasion, William had an appointment to meet with Dr. Hampton in the afternoon. However, his behavior during class that morning was extremely disruptive, and just before recess, Karen told him, "You're not going to get to see Dr. Hampton because that's a privilege." She insisted that he postpone his appointment until he had returned to her class and demonstrated appropriate behavior for a few minutes. William went off to recess, and apparently reported this exchange to Dr. Hampton, who soon came looking for Karen. Karen reported, "Dr. Hampton was *very* upset with me," and the psychologist made it clear that Karen should let William go to the scheduled appointment. Karen recalled, "I said to her, 'This behavior is really bad today, and I just don't know . . . if I feel comfortable giving him

Tips for New Teachers: Three Approaches to Management Problems

Management problems happen. Plan for them, as you would plan for a lesson with scripting, transitions, and contingencies. The goal should be to minimize disruption of instructional time while responding appropriately to situations that require attention. Here are three possibilities:

Plan A

(often suitable for minor and clear infractions such as tardiness, missing homework, talking out of turn, etc.)

● Confirm facts about infraction and accountable individual(s) as necessary.

● Be clear and unemotional in assigning predetermined penalty.

● Return quickly to instruction and try not to discuss the matter further.

Plan B

(often suitable for less clear infractions where there might be mitigating circumstances, uncertain or group responsibility, insufficient information about what happened or who was involved, etc.)

● Announce that a decision will be made later and return immediately to instruction.

● As soon as time permits, collect any available information.

● Consult with colleagues or administrators to get advice, if necessary.

● Make a decision and announce it publicly so that all students will know that there were consequences.

● If guilt cannot be determined, a phone call to parents of suspected participants to discuss unrelated matters (grades, attendance, upcoming events) can put students on notice.

Plan C

(often suitable when an incident is outside a teacher's jurisdiction, responsibility, or control)

● Acknowledge issue so students know that you are aware of it.

● Return to instructional activities immediately.

● If necessary, report the incident to administrators or other authorities.

> Worth Discussing: Tough Choices
>
> Every spring, you meet with the colleagues who teach at your grade level and the next one to make class assignments for the coming year. You lobby for the placements you feel will be most beneficial for your students. In your estimation, there is one weak teacher at the next grade level. She seems disorganized and unprepared, and you suspect that her classroom is not a great learning environment. Among your current students, there are a few very high achievers who would benefit from enrichment and accelerated instruction. There are a few students who struggle with reading and would benefit from intensive guided practice. Most of the students are in the middle, but you know that they, too, need motivating and appropriately tailored instruction to help them achieve at the highest levels possible. Some of your students will need to be placed in the weak teacher's class. What should you recommend?

the privilege of going to see you when he's acting this way.'" Dr. Hampton responded by asking, "Don't you understand that this is the healing process?" Karen remembered saying, "I understand that, and I know that he needs it more than anyone in my room, but I feel like I'm rewarding him" for poor behavior. According to Karen, Dr. Hampton argued in response that her sessions with William were not a privilege but "what he needs."

In reflecting on this incident, Karen expressed deep ambivalence. She said, "I think William needs to [talk with Dr. Hampton], but at the same time I'm kind of torn because it's a signal to him that you can meditate at your desk and roll on the floor and laugh in a really disruptive way at every little thing . . . and still get to go have this nice special time." While acknowledging real and profound needs in William that warrant his time with Dr. Hampton, Karen felt that "it's also a privilege for him to take time out of the classroom." She reported, "William loves going to her." Karen was concerned about being in conflict with Dr. Hampton because, as she noted, "It sets up a very unprofessional dynamic."

Karen has good reason to be concerned. Any dynamic that pits colleagues against each other with a student as the intermediary is bound to be unprofessional, if not adversarial. This confrontation hinges on questions of professional qualifications, life experience, and background: Who knows more about what William needs, the teacher or the psychologist? The perspectives that Dr. Hampton and Karen bring to bear on William's case are dramatically different, and each has merit. Dr. Hampton has more expertise in assisting students with special needs like William, but Karen spends much more time with him and may be more familiar with the particulars of his case. The therapy sessions may well be essential to "the healing process," but in a public school setting, a weekly appointment with an attentive and sympathetic adult can be a privilege, the stigma notwithstanding. Dr. Hampton may be an advocate for William and other students on her caseload, but Karen also must be an advocate for the rest of the students in her class. Like a grandparent, Dr. Hampton may choose to be indulgent and solely affirmative; given William's behavior and the needs of the other students, Karen cannot. Dr. Hampton sees William for one appointment each week, and Karen sees him all the rest of the school hours. Dr. Hampton is a *Dr.*, but Karen is a *Ms.*

In short, Karen's attempt at fairness leaves her confused and dissatisfied. She needed to respond to William's behavior with a defensible decision. She tried to, although Dr. Hampton clearly believed it was a misguided one. Importantly, Karen's decision appeared more forceful than it was. Her words were firm, but they masked deep uncertainty. By her own admission, she did not know what would help William. She did know that she felt she could not ignore his behavior during class that morning. When her good-faith attempt to respond appropriately to the situation was challenged by Dr. Hampton, Karen felt intimidated and full of self-recrimination. Although her process of making a professional judgment is reasonable, the contested outcome undermines her confidence, sense of efficacy, and authority. Despite her best efforts to be part of the solution, Karen confronts the possibility that she is just another part of the problem. This deflating prospect—accurate or not—can impair new teachers' competence by making them timid and tentative in making necessary judgments.

Integrity

Like fairness, integrity is a recurrent issue in classrooms. These teachers expressed the desire to be good educators and do right by their students. Believing that their actions were morally sound was an important part of their desired role as a force for good in the lives of young people. Aside from its moral appeal, integrity also has practical value. It helps a teacher to be and be perceived by others as fair, consistent, and upstanding in her judgments. That reputation enhances credibility with students, parents, and colleagues. However, for these new teachers, determining a moral course proved much more complicated than they had expected.

For example, Karen recounted that one day some agitated girls in her class came to her to report, "Isabel isn't a virgin anymore." Immediately, Karen said, "My alarms went off." She wondered, "Do I sit and have this little roundtable discussion about the state of Isabel's virginity, or as a teacher, is it my role to stay out of that? It was a very fine line." Karen had to respond immediately, since the girls were waiting, so she asked for more information. Later she said, "Isabel had this big grin on her face as she told

Tips for New Teachers: Saving Face, Fixing Mistakes

New teachers are very likely to make some misjudgments. When you do, admit it and try to make amends. Model for students a willingness to own up to errors. However, you need not abase yourself or surrender your authority. You can save face and still acknowledge a problem, especially if your response includes appropriate praise and appreciation as well as accountability. Consider the following approaches next time you need to undo your words or actions.

- "I need to think about this matter a little more. I'll let you know tomorrow what my position is. Until then . . ."

- "I appreciate the way that the class followed my instructions today. Unfortunately, I made a mistake on the assignment sheet. Please make the following correction and extend the due date until . . ."

- "After discussing this situation with my colleague(s), I have changed my mind . . ."

- "I thought about this problem last night, and I want to revise yesterday's decision . . ."

- "Next time this issue arises, you can expect . . ."

me what had happened" with a neighbor boy her age who attended another school. Relieved to learn that this incident was apparently not a case of statutory rape, Karen then remembered saying to Isabel:

I'm sure that you feel very uncomfortable sharing this and upset about what happened. It doesn't make you a bad person. It's just something for adults. It's not a thing that children—you know—should be doing. Did you tell your mom? Did she do anything about it? Do you need me to do anything for you? I'm sorry that this happened. I hope it doesn't happen again.

Karen recalled, "I didn't want to make her feel like 'Oh, you horrible, terrible, dirty child.' But at the same time, I didn't want to make her feel like it was okay. . . . It put me in a really awkward position." She explained to Isabel that she planned to call home and that she would report the incident to Child Protective Services (CPS). Then the girls started saying, "She could be *pregnant*. She could have *AIDS*." Karen recalled later, "I [wasn't] going to give a lecture on whether or not these things are possible." In spite of Karen's phone messages and notes sent home, the mother never responded.

Karen reported, "Finally, I just stopped." She also called CPS, and no action was taken since no adults were involved, but according to Karen, the staff did record the incident for future reference. In the end, Karen said, "I felt so uncomfortable, and I wasn't sure if I'd handled it right."

The actual events are hard to discern in all the euphemisms and hearsay. However, the issues raised—possible abuse or molestation, shame, victimization, curiosity about sexuality, communication with parents, jurisdiction of school or CPS personnel, pregnancy, AIDS—are issues with real weight and consequences. They may be particularly material in poorer urban areas where financial resources, education, and access to medical care or legal recourse may be scarce. For some, linguistic barriers may preclude effective communication. Particularly within immigrant communities, the displacement of families from cultures left behind may leave children rudderless in negotiating early adolescence and their parents uncertain what guidance is appropriate in the new setting. In other words, these girls approached Karen with a shocking story, and her response mattered.

Her concern about doing the "right" thing may be telling. Like most people, Karen wanted to be confident that her behavior was at least defensible and preferably laudable. Yet her mixed feelings about her principal and about Dr. Hampton, the psychologist, may have made Karen less inclined to seek needed help from them. In this situation, determining the right thing to do, or even the best thing under the circumstances, is very difficult, in part because the circumstances are so shadowy. Isabel's account requires a response on both legal and moral grounds. Karen is obligated to contact CPS, and although she fulfills her legal obligation, the experience leaves her less than fully satisfied. In simply making a record of the report, CPS does not deal directly with Isabel, leaving a gap that Karen feels compelled to try to fill. Her moral obligations are much more difficult to discharge. Her immediate words to Isabel are intended to provide assurance, guidance, and the promise of assistance, but they leave Karen feeling uneasy.

The girls' subsequent concerns about pregnancy and AIDS are certainly legitimate, but Karen determines them to be beyond the scope of this conversation. Given no warning or preparation, it seems reasonable to postpone, at least, any discussion of these topics. Further, there is a broader context to consider that requires more reflection. Karen described parts of the school community as "very church-oriented," and she felt concerned about violating community norms with a frank conversation about sexually transmitted diseases. Karen wanted to pursue the appropriate course of action, but she did not know what it was, and she felt alone in trying to discern it.

Ultimately, Karen decided, "Calming kids is what I need to do rather than give any opinion or any sweeping generalization. Just calming kids and making sure they're okay." Refraining from giving opinions can be its own virtue. It allows Karen to feel respectful of community norms and to

Worth Discussing: Charged Topics

Every community has polarizing issues, and teachers inevitably are drawn into debate about them through policy discussions, curriculum decisions, and informal conversations. What are the polarizing issues in your school community? When an elementary student, secondary student, parent, or colleague raises these issues, how will you respond?

School Issues

- Ability grouping
- Multicultural curriculum
- Required readings
- Religious holiday observances
- The Pledge of Allegiance
- Dress code

Policy Issues

- Affirmative Action
- English-only laws
- Environmental issues
- Energy issues
- Civil liberties

Health and Safety Issues

- Sexuality
- AIDS education
- Abortion
- Abuse
- Drugs
- Guns

sidestep sure controversy. However, Karen clearly had reservations about her stance. While logical and practical, it lacks convincing moral forceful-ness. In fact, her stance may be one of the reasons that some parents find public schools objectionable. Teaching is a moral enterprise, but because public schools are an arm of the government and not of any specific religion or philosophy, moral instruction must be somewhat oblique and imprecise. Karen is left to mull her unhappy predicament: Perhaps she should have said more, and preferably, she might have said less.

For new teachers, the desire for professional integrity pulls in different directions. Karen is caught in the middle. She wants to be a force for good in her students' lives but hopes to avoid confrontations over ethical differences. She wants to affirm and encourage all her students but wishes that they would behave in ways that she finds appropriate (Ruddick, 1980). In essence, she struggles to find a sense of integrity that can be rigorous and meaningful but is unlikely to make anyone feel bad. It may be that young people are particularly idealistic about avoiding compromise in moral issues and that some women are particularly concerned about a moral vision that is as inclusive and free of conflict as possible (Gilligan, 1982). In any case, for new teachers like Karen, contradictory expectations about integrity may make exercising professional judgment difficult.

Jurisdiction

While fairness and integrity are clearly moral concepts, jurisdiction is a more mundane matter. The moral dilemmas that surround it are more subtle, but their repercussions are profound. Ideally, the faculty of a school would share a common philosophy about important matters like curriculum, evaluation, and discipline. It may be that the most crucial area of agreement is discipline. Inconsistencies among different teachers and classes in matters of curriculum and evaluation can be frustrating and confusing, but they are unlikely to undermine the effectiveness of the whole school the way inconsistent discipline can. Presumably, each teacher is responsible for addressing any incidents, fights, or disputes that arise in a classroom of her own. However, problems also crop up in common areas of the school: the halls, the yard, the bathrooms, and the cafeteria. Maintaining a sense of order in these common areas is difficult, in part, because there are conflicting jurisdictions. When there is a fracas, the classroom teacher, the yard duty teacher, any adult witness, or an administrator might respond, but overlapping jurisdictions sometimes mean that no one is truly responsible. A new teacher who chooses to make common area discipline one of her battles engages in an important service to the school. Even so, she may find that she does herself a disservice.

For example, Karen supervised lunch in the cafeteria on a day when there had been an assembly with helium balloons. After lunch, she watched a girl whom she did not know hitting other children with the balloons. When Karen approached and asked her to stop, the girl continued and even batted the balloon at Karen, hitting her. At that point, Karen marched her down to the office. Since no senior administrators were available, Karen described the situation to the administrative assistant and then returned to her post in the cafeteria. Later, she explained that she hoped not to return to the office that afternoon because she did not want to know if the girl had not been disciplined. Specifically, if there had been no follow-up consequences assigned by an administrator, Karen did not want the girl to know that Karen was aware of this omission. Under those circumstances, Karen would have an implied obligation to pursue the matter herself, and she did not want to invest more time in it.

A week after this incident, Karen knew little about what had happened to the girl. She reported:

> I asked the secretary if she still wanted me to call [the girl's] mother . . . and she said, "No, you don't." And I said, "Did someone call her mother, or how is this being handled?" and she said, "The substitute is going to write a note to her teacher."

Karen had delivered the girl to the office with the understanding that the girl's behavior violated some fundamental standard of student behavior. Instead, she found that her concerns were met with indifference. She doubted that any consequences would ever come to this student on account of her behavior. Karen felt frustrated and chastened for trying to be conscientious.

Teachers may find that when they intervene in discipline matters in the common areas of the school with students who are not in their classes, they create problems for themselves. If the issue cannot be resolved at the scene, embroiled students may be sent to the office for further discipline. Busy with their own primary duties, administrators may not follow through consistently on—or even know about—matters referred to them. They are likely to have only sketchy accounts of the problem and may be in an awkward position to adjudicate the case. The teachers, however, have moved on, returning to their classes. They may seek no further involvement other than confirmation that the matter was addressed in an instructive and fair way. In some instances, neither administrator nor teacher follows through, each assuming that the other owns the problem. To complicate matters, there is a de facto statute of limitations in schools. When lunchtime or the class hour or the school day ends, so does the opportunity for meaningful and timely disciplinary action. The student easily slips out, often incurring only the dubious penalties of missing class and getting attention from the secretary.

To the degree that a student sent to the office by a teacher faces no repercussions for inappropriate behavior, that student has beaten the system. The real loser is the referring teacher, who appears weak and ineffective. It is in everyone's collective interest but no one's individual interest to intervene. Given these dynamics, there is a powerful disincentive for teachers to intervene in the common areas of the school. Although new teachers may not yet know it, the teacher is punished for her diligence by having to invest the time to follow up or else lose face. Intervention in the common areas makes sense only in an organization where all of the adults share a philosophy about discipline, where ownership and discipline procedures are clearly defined, and where communication can occur quickly and accurately. Few schools meet these criteria. As teachers learn to ignore rude or aggressive behavior, it becomes acceptable and eventually normal. The moral foundations of school life, particularly respect for other people and property, deteriorate.

The net result of this willful blindness is a perception by students that the common areas are their domain, free of adult supervision or jurisdiction. A teacher like Karen who does intervene in that area may be the exception on the staff and be perceived by students and administrators alike as overreacting or interfering in matters that are none of her business. The sense here is that it is the teacher who is out of line rather than the student. Inexperienced teachers are particularly vulnerable to these kinds of problems because they may be too new to perceive the degree of involvement administrators are willing to have in discipline matters. Administrators may not be able or willing to intervene in these issues, they may not trust the judgment of the new teacher, and they may be wary of powerful parents backing a student or of unfavorable publicity resulting from the incident. The relatively low status of a new teacher in the school—perhaps especially a woman with a discipline problem on her hands—may make administrator support particularly unlikely. On the other hand, if inexperienced teachers withdraw from common area supervision, they lose face as students watch them tolerate inappropriate behavior and the campus atmosphere declines.

Young women teachers may be particularly prone to having their concerns about common areas ignored. As women, they may have legitimate reason for heightened concerns about physical safety (Tannen, 1994; Wilson & Kelling, 1982) and about respect for their authority. To the degree that they have no strong alliances among the administrators, are perceived as unrealistic in their expectations of student behavior, or are unable to dispense with management issues on their own, they have only the official channels of support to help them. In fact, teachers who find support in the office often have more informal avenues to assistance. Specifically, they may have cultivated networks with the administrators who are most likely to be able to help, and sometimes more important, with their secretaries.

Secretaries—often women—are key players in schools, as in many other organizations. In matters of jurisdiction, they can be particularly powerful. Karen delivered the girl to the office with the hope that she would be called to account for her deeds in a stern conversation with an administrator that would lead to disciplinary measures. Instead, Karen sus-

---

Tips for New Teachers: Discipline Without Administrators

When new teachers have classroom management problems, they sometimes turn immediately to administrators for help. Although administrators may be valuable resources, there are at least two problems with this approach to discipline: (a) administrators are busy, and (b) new teachers need to develop their own authority. The following tips may help new teachers respond to both.

- Discuss discipline strategies with administrators *before* you have a problem on your hands. Assume that administrators are often out of their offices or in meetings. Do not send a child to see an administrator without a prearranged protocol for such situations. Coordinate with the secretary or other office staff, if appropriate.

- If possible, make contact with each child's parent(s) during the first month of school. Speak with parents at orientation meetings, Back-to-School Nights, or on the phone. Introduce yourself, briefly describe your plans for the year, and express interest in each child. If possible, make only positive comments. Set a tone of cooperation.

- When problems arise, call the parent(s) immediately. Explain the problem and consequence. Assure the parent(s) that you are taking steps to help the child make progress, and if possible, offer suggestions for reinforcement at home.

- Form a standing arrangement to send recalcitrant students (one at a time) to sit quietly in the back of a nearby colleague's classroom for ten minutes. The change of venue often allows for a fresh start without administrator involvement.

- Determine and publicize behavior standards and consequences, and then try to solve problems within your own classroom. You will be more authoritative in the eyes of your students, and administrators will appreciate not being drawn into every conflict that arises.

---

pected that her complaint was undermined by the secretary with some informal counseling, a gentle reprimand, and a reprieve. In some cases, this person is the only one who knows that a student is in the office, waiting. The secretary sometimes fills the gap left by the absence of the teacher and administrator, and she may offer encouragement, advice, and a pass to return to class. If she is sympathetic, she may set up a dynamic where she is the student's defense counsel against the teacher's prosecution. Significantly, when Karen inquired about the case, it was the secretary who told her that the matter would be resolved. She may be protecting Karen's time by freeing her from further obligation, but she also may be shutting Karen out in order to mitigate the punishment, if any, for the student. In this case, the secretary functions not only as defense counsel but also as judge.

In brief, outside a teacher's immediate class, jurisdiction may be hard to discern. New teachers, especially if they are tainted—rightly or wrongly—with associations of poor classroom management, may have a hard time finding support for their disciplinary actions outside, not to mention inside, their classrooms. As new teachers develop professional judgment, they must learn to choose the battles they are willing to fight so as not to lay waste their powers.

Sound professional judgment in teaching requires moral undergirding. However, there is no formula to guide a teacher through moral matters. On the contrary, teaching is about a kind of morality that is particularly difficult to pin down because it involves the special obligations of a stewardship over young people. Hugh Sockett argued:

> Educational programs of all kinds should aspire to contribute to human betterment without being outrageously unrealistic and with the knowledge that a school is not a replica of society. A moral ethos in the school, its character as a just and fair institution, is essential for children's social, civic, and moral growth. (1993, p. 82)

Good teachers need to care enough to feel invested in their students' academic and social development, but not so much that they forestall natural consequences of student behavior or manipulate standards to guarantee pleasing results. They need to care about their individual students, but also about each class unit, the school, the profession, and themselves. Paradoxically, in attending to competing demands, "[a teacher] may also need to neglect in order to care" (Sockett, 1993, p. 79).

Experienced teachers come to know their core values and beliefs through responding to real situations with actions. They refine strategies for addressing problems. New teachers may be caught off guard by the fact that conflicts arise, by their timing, by the players, by the potency of the emotions, by the consequences, by the absence of administrative or parental support, and perhaps most disturbingly, by the moral ambiguity of the alternatives. Professional judgment requires a clear-eyed understanding of the factors as well as the confidence to make a choice and live with the fallout. In addition, if a new teacher is to be competent, she has to find a way to reconcile her sense of morality with efficacy in the school context. Morality can be strategic and still be moral. In fact, it may be that in order to be moral in an institution and a bureaucracy, one must be at least somewhat strategic. Otherwise, the best of intentions may profit nothing.

Tips for New Teachers: Behaviors That Allow Good Things to Happen

1. Speak slowly, clearly, and calmly. Project into corners.

2. Give explicit instructions. When feasible, write them down for students. Divide complex tasks into component parts.

3. Be aware. Always scan the room. Use your peripheral vision.

4. Move around. Position yourself in different locations, including the back.

5. Plan for transitions between activities.

6. Return to students who have been disciplined within the hour. Offer them opportunities to participate in productive ways.

7. Assign students' seats. Rotate them during the year.

CONCLUSION

Teaching is Karen's job, not her life. This statement might be an embarrassing attribution, given the glory lauded on teachers whose lives and jobs seem indistinguishable. Teachers who are held up as exemplars rarely go home at 4 p.m., even if the day began early. However, part of developing professional judgment is reaching a degree of comfort in establishing boundaries. Having no boundaries preserves the illusion of a vast, all-encompassing commitment to students, colleagues, and the educational endeavor, but in failing to prioritize, it undermines the moral enterprise of teaching. As well, it sets a dangerous and unfair standard for all teachers. It may be particularly unfair to women, who frequently shoulder a disproportionate amount of caregiving obligations outside of employment. Further, to the degree that women teachers are subjected to ideals of selfless care for others often associated with mothers (Acker, 1995; Ruddick, 1980), they may be particularly susceptible to feeling discouraged and demoralized when they fall short. Some research suggests that women, in particular, find public school teaching stressful (Calabrese & Anderson, 1986; Martin, 1990; Robertson, 1992). Boundaries help protect the relationships and activities outside of school that can be essential for mental and physical health.

For new teachers who are idealistic, the notion of boundaries itself may be disappointing. It can be deflating to come to know that helping others is not simply a matter of responding without reservation to any demonstrated need. Making careful, deliberate decisions about how and when to

> ### Worth Discussing: Career Angst
>
> On her morning commute, Karen drove through a busy financial center and saw women her own age on their way to work in high-rise offices. She described feeling a little jealous of their "gorgeous clothes," which Karen said she could not afford and that would be totally impractical for teaching, anyway. She reported that her father told her, "I could see you teaching at the college level." This comment, with its implication that working with children was not worthy of her gifts, was painful to Karen. Nonetheless, her feelings about the profession were undeniably fractured. She said, "Teachers are these amazing people who work really, really hard," but "I'm not like these people." It is a dual view of teaching, a belief in its possible power and importance as well as its potential for mindless, custodial care from people lacking in ability or ambition. How would you respond to Karen?

expend the precious commodities of time, attention, and energy may allow a new teacher to concentrate her efforts where they are most effective, preserve the quality of her private life, and allow greater longevity in a field pocked by high attrition.

This is the anatomy of professional judgment: It is the heart and mind and stomach to make difficult decisions about the worthiness and probable effectiveness of any given alternative. For new teachers, accumulating the insight and experience necessary for this kind of judgment may seem painstakingly slow. Those who are new adults may have come into the responsibilities, but not always the full status, of majority. They may not have imagined that helping students and trying to make a difference could be so complicated. "The sheer complexity and agonizing difficulty of choosing well" (Nussbaum, 1990, p. 55) can be unexpected and paralyzing. Worse, rationality is flawed. Unstable preferences, changing circumstances, and misinterpretation of events undermine the judgment of even experienced professionals (March, 1988). Yet while professional judgment may be an imperfect tool, perhaps particularly in the hands of new teachers, it is essential for effective teaching. Cultivating it through observation, discussion, and reflection—both formal and informal—is one of the first and greatest steps toward competence a new teacher can take.

7 Julie

Affirmation and Attainment

Every day's a success.

Julie

Teaching is middle-class work (Lortie, 1975; Webb, 1985) done primarily by white women (Feistritzer, 1990; Meek, 1998). In many areas, and certainly in this school district, the students are of diverse backgrounds in terms of race, language, ethnicity, religion, and social class. In some situations, the teachers' and students' backgrounds may be fairly homogeneous, but it is more likely, particularly in an urban setting, that they will be quite disparate (Weiner, 1993). While homogeneity of students and teachers may be unlikely in public schools, it offers an interesting contrasting view of one teacher's experience.

A CASE STUDY OF HOMOGENEITY

Of the six teachers in this group, Julie was a clear outlier. She taught in a school atypical of this district. Ensconced in an affluent pocket of the city, its student population generally came from wealthy, well-educated white families in the area. Despite a space crisis that crippled some of the other schools, this one had not only a library and a computer lab, but also an on-site child care center open ten hours a day. Consequently, this teaching environment was unusual. Julie had come to it indirectly. After graduating from college, she had worked at a "boring" job in advertising for a year or two until she concluded that she was "not a desk person." Since earning a teaching credential, she had taught for four years, three of them at this school.

Meet the Teacher: Julie

Age: 28

Education: B.A. Psychology and Business

Professional Training: Teaching credential

Number of Years Teaching: 4

Grade Level: 1st

Class Size: 20

Special Assignments: None

School Enrollment: 500

Schoolwide Eligibility for Subsidized Lunch: 5%

Schoolwide Ethnicity: 60% Caucasian, 20% African American, 20% Other

Schoolwide Achievement Scores Compared With National Average: Significantly above

In many ways, Julie was the quintessential primary grade teacher. She was slim and attractive, organized, friendly, and calm. Her work clothes were sporty but distinctly feminine. Her penmanship was impeccable. She did not seem to raise her voice ever. Julie considered her youth an asset. She said, "[The parents were] happy that I was young because they thought I would have a more fresh approach." In addition, Julie believed that "it helps to be young" because the kids "identify more with your style, age, and dress." While she felt that her youth and gender were "mostly an advantage," she qualified her assessment to specify that "definitely the environment makes it an advantage."

At this school, teaching in the primary grades is largely about affirmation and encouragement. Goals are clear, measurable, and given the context, attainable. The administrators, teachers, parents, students, and community members seem to share an understanding of the purposes and means of public school. The children should learn to read. They should learn some basic math. Generally, they do, and often with bravura. "Every day's a success," Julie said. "At first, they couldn't read." By spring, every child in the class was reading, many with exceptional facility, obvious enjoyment, and satisfaction. Learning happened here, routinely and uneventfully. Julie reported that "it has always been true of [her]" to want to please everyone, and most of the time, she came pretty close, given this environment. Consequently, Julie reported, "I've never had any problems" with parents or colleagues.

Parent Expectations

The parents at Julie's school were more visible than at any of the other schools in which teachers in this study worked. Twice a week, parent volunteers were scheduled to assist Julie during reading time. Since the class was already split for reading groups, there was a ratio of three adults to ten children, and every student had an opportunity to read orally to an adult. At the spring Parent Night, every child had at least one parent attend, and most had both. Of the twenty children in the class, nineteen lived with both parents. While most of the parents worked, they figured out ways to be available to help with holiday parties and to drive on field trips. Julie had the choice of taking a district school bus on one field trip each year or else buying supplies with the money saved by not going. She bought the supplies and went on numerous field trips anyway using parent drivers. She bypassed the district processes and went directly to the people who cared most about the field trips: the parents. They were not gatekeepers but rather facilitators. When Julie said, "I couldn't do it without the parents," she spoke the truth. Julie was not limited by the constraints that other new teachers in the study encountered, in part because there were sufficient resources for her needs. Further, the parents rallied around her. Whether her status was sufficient or not, theirs certainly was.

At some level, Julie understood and fulfilled the role of teacher that these parents envisioned. When a father approached her at Parent Night and asked what he could do to help his son, Julie responded, "Handwriting." The father nodded his head knowingly and moved on. Whether or not the boy has poor handwriting, Julie's answer is brilliant. A proper teacher knows a student's weaknesses. To say to a conscientious parent that his child has no areas of weakness is tantamount to admitting professional negligence. However, to identify a serious or debilitating concern, particularly on this social occasion with other parents milling around, is potentially alarming and embarrassing. Handwriting is the perfect answer. It is specific and benign. High-status professionals sometimes have bad handwriting. It is a mechanical and motor problem, not a conceptual or intellectual deficiency. The understanding implicit in this context is that Julie is to make sure that there are no serious academic deficiencies or that existing ones are corrected swiftly. There is an unarticulated but pervasive awareness that life chances and academic performance are correlated. Julie's role is to stay the course for children presumed to be headed toward exceptional opportunities in each.

To illustrate, Julie described the annual administration of a new statewide standardized test. Shortly after the test, she explained to the parent

Tips for New Teachers: Appropriate Communication With Parents

Teachers and parents are partners—not colleagues—in education. Professional competence includes an understanding of which subjects are productive and appropriate to discuss with parents and which are not.

Discuss With Parents:

1. Praise or concerns about their children

2. Positive assessments of your colleagues

3. Topics of current faculty debate and objective descriptions of faculty positions

4. Specific concerns that parent or citizen groups can help address (needed resources, volunteer opportunities, campus safety, local fund-raising, bond issues, voter initiatives, etc.)

Don't Discuss With Parents:

1. Praise or concerns about other children in the class

2. Unflattering assessments of your colleagues

3. Subjective appraisals of your colleagues' positions in faculty debates

4. Gripes, interpersonal complaints, strictly administrative matters, or other issues that parents need not know about and cannot or should not influence

volunteers that the math portion had been quite difficult. Julie had responded by giving the students extra time, in violation of the test instructions. While her actions undermine the validity of the test, they increase the odds that students will score well. The parents nodded approvingly. One mother bemoaned the use of standardized testing in the primary grades. These parents have no reason to question the validity of the test, its biases, or its appropriateness in evaluating students' academic abilities. In differentiating their children, it serves their interests, whether they are aware of it or not. No wonder they complain about the test in a rhetorical way. These parents expect their children to learn to take it and do well, even as they bemoan its encroachment into their notions of untroubled childhood.

Although Julie enjoys good rapport with parents at her school, she does not imagine that they are appropriate professional confidants. They are a powerful constituency and a potentially manipulative one. One way Julie can define her sphere of influence and resist being completely dominated by parents is by controlling the flow of information to them. For example, in May, when Julie's teaching assignment for the coming year was finalized, she feigned ignorance about it because she did not want the parents to start mobilizing. She knew that given all the available information, they would begin assessing the available teachers at each grade level and jockeying for placements. The relationship between Julie and the parents is cordial and supportive. They seem genuinely appreciative of each other. However, while the relationship is clearly not adversarial, it is not an unguarded partnership, either.

Julie understands the parents' expectations well enough to casually pass on information that flatters her in their eyes—even if it is technically inappropriate, such as the standardized test procedure—and to withhold information that could make her the object of scrutiny, such as her future teaching assignment. She knows what to tell them and what not to tell them. Like a savvy spokeswoman, she controls the flow of information and scripts the leaks for her own purposes. In this setting, the generally shared understanding of the purposes of school and the function of a teacher minimize the confrontation in the classroom and any angst about doing the right thing. Julie is well situated to be authoritative, and she conveys that sense. The structures in place at her school, the resources, and the population make it possible for her to do her work and see evidence of success. She is consistently supported by parents and administrators, and as a result, looks confident and competent. Her job is clearly defined—teach reading, writing, math, and a little science and social studies—and she can proceed with surety. The match between teacher and parent expectations makes Julie's experience fairly smooth.

Administration

Julie's experience with administration parallels her positive experience with the parents. Alone among the study teachers, Julie praised her principal, Clara. "She is great," Julie said. A Chinese American woman, Clara might enjoy special rapport with the many Chinese families in the school, and she certainly shared the rigorous academic expectations that characterized this school's parents and teachers. She used her administrative role to clear the path for teachers to focus on these priorities. According to Julie, Clara "shields new teachers, protects them." As well, she is not autocratic but "brings any decisions to us all and gets our input." Julie reported that Clara handled a lot of cumbersome paperwork herself, including writing the school's Program Quality Review (PQR). Interestingly, when the principal did the same thing at Beth's school, Beth felt that he was being furtive and negligent, if not dishonest. Clara handled the same assignment in a

> ## Tips for New Teachers: Preempting Conflict
>
> Some conflicts are inevitable. Others can be avoided with careful planning and skillful redirection. Here are a few ways to minimize unnecessary conflict:
>
> - Generate and distribute written copies of policies, assignments, and calendars. Anticipate and include issues such as late assignments, makeup work, behavior, tardies, and absences.
>
> - Make your policies reasonable and a little flexible, but then don't make exceptions. ("I'm sorry that your homework was sucked into a vortex. I'll look forward to getting it tomorrow, but it will be counted late.")
>
> - Be sympathetic without being indulgent. ("I've had papers disappear into the vortex, too. It's frustrating. Unfortunately, the assignment is still due today.")
>
> - Assume that everyone else has amnesia, and document all phone calls and conferences. Photocopy grade book and attendance records regularly.
>
> - Give people advance warning. Administrators, parents, and students need to know if trouble is brewing. A low grade or significant disciplinary action should not come as a surprise.
>
> - Use appropriate humor as often as possible.

way that made teachers like Julie feel grateful. While the personal styles of the principals and teachers no doubt influence these interpretations, it may also be that the sense of shared understanding at Julie's school allows the PQR to be written by one person in a way that feels inclusive of the faculty. Perhaps the principal's and teachers' visions at Julie's school are not so disparate as to require cobbling together dissenting opinions.

For Julie, "Strong administration [had] made all the difference" in a pleasant work environment. She said, "Clara keeps us really well informed." As well, there was no public address system, and there were virtually no interruptions to class. A surprise assembly was unimaginable to Julie. Jurisdictional disputes did not seem to be a problem. Clara ran detention, and referring teachers simply left a note on her desk and sent a copy to the student's classroom teacher. According to Julie, by "setting up a clear course of action," misbehavior was nipped early, and overall the campus stayed calm and orderly. Inservice meetings occurred monthly at Julie's school, instead of weekly as at most other schools in the district. At those meetings, the principal gave the "lowdown" and got staff input. Since students performed well at this school, morale was fairly high, and inservice time was sometimes allotted for atypical purposes, such as packing up classrooms before some summer construction work. Julie felt adequately represented at school site meetings. "I never felt like I had to find some vehicle to get my voice heard at all," she remarked. However, beyond her school, she does not venture into district politics. "I hate that stuff," she said. Particularly with regard to the strike, Julie said, "I didn't feel like my little voice [would make] any difference." As a new teacher, Julie was assigned a mentor teacher from her school and meetings were held there. Attendance by new teachers from other schools was poor.

Supervising adults was no problem for Julie. The instructional aide assigned to her room, Miranda, was hired by the school PTA rather than the district. Consequently, she was accountable to Julie, the principal, and the PTA parents, and her charter was very clear. She was to do the teacher's bidding. According to Julie, Miranda was a "bulletin board genius" who made sure that Julie's walls were covered with colorful and timely artwork, calendars, and seasonal decorations. At a school where at least some parents might be able to afford private school tuition, the staff concerned itself with public relations, and this attention to detail was not trivial. Miranda also worked with students or helped with grading, and if she finished early, she would sweep or clean desks. She was "great" and "super reliable," Julie reported, and furthermore every aide she had worked with at this school had been terrific. Assessment was uneventful for Julie. Presumably, she could evaluate Miranda with glowing praise.

Evaluation of Julie's performance was not a source of frustration, either. She said, "[I] can't divulge too many secrets," and "[I] don't want to get Clara in trouble." Since it was Julie's third year in the district, she was supposed to be observed formally multiple times in preparation for a tenure decision about her. Instead, Clara popped in periodically when she was in the vicinity. She looked at the bulletin boards and did not stay for a full lesson. In this way, Julie explained, Clara minimized "the time-consuming waste" of the district evaluation. Julie said, "The evaluations are always great. I keep [them] in my file for the future."

Her principal's behavior, if accurately reported, is interesting. It may be that Clara knows enough about Julie not to be concerned about her teaching. Julie looked the part and reflected the school's overall philosophy. It may be that Clara knew that the paperwork was time-consuming and meant little, so she tried not to spend unnecessary time on it. It may be that she wanted to express her confidence and appreciation to her staff by not troubling them with empty paperwork. It may be that she could treat evaluations as formalities because parents effectively would force out the weakest teachers. The motives may not matter to Julie. She ended up with minimal hassle, positive feedback, and a sense of trust and confidence. The

> **Worth Discussing: Teachers, Race, and Student Achievement**
>
> One of the realities of public education is the intermixing of students from diverse backgrounds. The attendant consequences of shared learning, shared play, and a more sophisticated understanding of our pluralistic society are an invaluable part of this education.
>
> However, some recent research suggests that students perform significantly better when placed in classes with teachers of their own racial backgrounds (Dee, 2001). Given the diversity of most American schools, how can administrators and teachers promote both social understanding and maximum academic achievement?

underlying assumption at Julie's school is one of agreement and competence. Given that orientation, evaluations attract little attention. If anything, complacency characterizes the process.

CONCLUSION

When asked what she would change about her school, Julie replied, "Nothing." She added her best advice to a new teacher: "Look for the right situation." Her situation seems to have been a happy match for her. However, in spite of Julie's rosy assessment of the setting, there were hints of problems. In general, the conflicts seemed to focus on people who were outside of this dominant understanding of the school and its function. More specifically, conflicts seemed to arise most readily around the people who were not affluent white professionals or their children. The next chapter discusses the role that race, ethnicity, and class can play in the development and resolution of these conflicts.

8 Unpredictable Outcomes
Race, Ethnicity, and Class

When a significant difference exists between the students' culture and the school's culture, teachers can easily misread students' aptitudes, intent, or abilities.

L. Delpit

Shawn was one of two African American children in Julie's class. A student with special needs, he was the lowest achiever, by far. The other African American boy had attention deficit hyperactivity disorder (ADHD), Julie reported. According to Julie, Shawn had made a lot of progress, but he was still far behind. He alienated others and interrupted a lot. Julie recommended that he repeat the same grade again next year, but his parents declined. During a partnered math activity about money, the white girl paired with Shawn chided him for not writing his name exactly in the corner of his paper, mentioning casually, "He's not very smart." She remarked offhandedly that Shawn had to go to a special class. In response, Shawn argued strongly, and incorrectly, that each denomination of coin had the same value. Julie mentioned that Shawn's younger brother also had been recommended for retention the next year. She reported that his mother worked days and his father worked nights. In a parking lot full of expensive imports and sport-utility vehicles, Shawn's father drove a notably older car. Julie suspected that the family lived outside the attendance area for the school and had secured enrollment by using a false address or some other equivocation.

The little information Julie provided about Shawn suggests a potentially complicated scenario. In her version of events, Shawn is a boy with

> **Cultural Dynamics: Rash Judgments**
>
> New teachers must guard against making unfair generalizations about students based on race, ethnicity, or social class. Sociologist Philippe Bourgois wrote, "Tangible markers like accent and clothing combine with subtler forms of expression such as eye contact, body language, play styles, and attention spans to persuade the agents of a mainstream, middle-class, white-dominated bureaucracy that a particular child is a disciplinary problem, emotionally disturbed, or of low intelligence" (1995, p. 176).

learning difficulties and behavior problems. His skills are deficient, his behavior is disruptive, and his social interactions with other students are sometimes awkward, if not charged. In ignoring the teachers' advice about retention, the parents seem uncooperative. The father's night job and older car, both anomalies in this school, confirm the family's metaphorical outsider status and make Julie wonder if the parents might be literal outsiders, enrolling their children through stealth or fraud.

Julie's recounting of facts and speculation is disconcerting. Both of the African American students in her class have been diagnosed, either formally or informally, with deficiencies. The difference in race between these boys and the other children is obvious. Differences in ethnicity may be implied in some of the behavioral and social conflicts. Julie suspects a difference in social class. In any case, Shawn does not fit in readily. Perhaps another year in the same grade would help that problem, along with any academic difficulties, but perhaps it would not. It might be as likely to exacerbate them as Shawn grows bigger and older than his classmates and consequently is perceived as duller and less able because he will not become more like them.

THE DIVERSITY DIVIDE

When new teachers work in urban public schools, they inevitably encounter a profound and baffling conundrum: In education, diversity is both irrelevant and central. It is irrelevant in the sense that knowledge is not bounded by culture, but it is tremendously important in shaping the social context in which that knowledge is constructed, valued, and transferred. Diversity is central to education, every situation has the potential for some partiality, and caring for other people's children often means something dramatically different from caring for children who are literally or culturally one's own (Delpit, 1995). Many teachers may encounter unanticipated bumps when they teach students who are fundamentally unlike themselves.

If young white women choose teaching with the hope of working with young people in a socially or politically significant endeavor and with an orientation of care, they may be particularly well situated to reach out to students from backgrounds unlike their own. However, if they imagine that their care is sufficient to render real and profound differences of race, ethnicity, and class irrelevant, they may overestimate their powers, underestimate the obstacles, or both. If they view themselves as agents of good or emphasize their own institutional roles as helpers, they may be surprised to discover that others may perceive them as patronizing, disrespectful, or weak. Patronizing behavior implies a status difference that may be singularly hard to accept from a woman, perhaps especially if she is white. Perceived disrespect from a woman, particularly a young one, may be experienced as exceptionally demeaning (Bourgois, 1995).

When these teachers work in urban schools, they face both the distinct demands of those settings and the chasm that can separate their own backgrounds from their new work environment. Big-city districts frequently have large, established bureaucracies that function to bring uniform practices and impartiality to the individual schools. At the same time, these schools are filled with children who are more likely than their suburban or rural peers to have particular educational needs associated with recent immigration, poverty, or racial minority status. The combination of inflexible processes with a dramatic range of student needs frequently makes teacher adaptation to individuals prohibitively costly in terms of time, energy, and resources (Weiner, 1993).

The boundaries separating race, ethnicity, and class can be blurry and artificial, and there is significant overlap among them. The remaining sections of this chapter describe the interaction of diverse student populations with the white middle-class women teachers in this study.

Race

Race is an inescapable part of classroom interaction, and teachers ignore it at their own—and their students'—peril (Ladson-Billings, 1994; Paley, 1979). White teachers may be particularly uncomfortable acknowledging differences in race and may prefer to adopt a color-blind stance (Ladson-Billings, 1994). Regardless of the teacher's stance, race matters, and the students know it.

For example, in a previous year, Paula had taught an African American girl named Keisha. Paula explained, "[Keisha knew] how to push my buttons." In an attempt at positive discipline, Paula offered to reward her for good behavior by taking her to McDonald's for a hamburger. Instead, Keisha asked if she could see where Paula lived, and eventually Paula did

---

Worth Discussing: Other People's Children

Madeleine Grumet noted, "Few of us would excuse our own children from their futures with the grace and understanding we extend to other people's children" (1988, p. 173). Think of a student in your class who is not making good progress toward a future that includes desirable options. What immediate step(s) can you take to help? What long-term plans can you initiate?

---

take her there. According to Paula, when Keisha saw the one-bedroom apartment, she was in awe of the amount of space and said, "Wow! You live here by yourself? My whole family lives in a place like this." Shortly after this visit, Keisha transferred to a class taught by an African American woman, explaining to Paula, "There aren't enough black people in this class."

Similarly, Paula found that her interactions with parents from other racial backgrounds were sometimes awkward. She wanted to believe that she and the parents were "equals [in a] partnership" focused on student achievement. Instead, she felt that many of her students' parents, particularly the fathers, were guarded or uncomfortable in talking with her. According to Paula, the fathers with whom she interacts are mostly employed, working-class men. She is a white-collar professional, albeit one with relatively low status. She is white. She has tremendous power over their children most of the day during much of the year. As a result, Paula and these fathers and mothers are not true peers. Her notion of a partnership might never occur to them, or, if it did, might be dismissed summarily as ridiculous. Clearly, a basic teacher-parent interaction is complicated here by differences in race, ethnicity, and class.

Schools can only reflect their larger societies, and schools' problems of racial difference mirror those elsewhere. For example, the relationships between white teachers and urban youth may parallel the relationships between white employers and urban employees (Bourgois, 1995). Specifically, urban students in schools may face many of the same difficulties that they face in the workplace, including discrimination and cultural misunderstanding (Jencks, 1992).

In a multicultural metropolis like the San Francisco Bay Area, there are more than just a few races represented in the schools. In addition to African Americans and whites, there are sizable proportions of Asians, Latinos, and Pacific Islanders, among others. Each of these large categories includes a host of distinctive subgroups. In fact, white students in this school district, as elsewhere in California, are a numerical minority. However, schools persist as largely white institutions in terms of values, culture, and priorities

(Delpit, 1995). Consequently, race remains the most obvious and blunt marker of one's place in the school system. For new teachers who are white, their association with the dominance of the mainstream may lead to perceptions of hostility, insensitivity, or indifference to students of other racial backgrounds. In an urban, multicultural setting, few associations could be more damaging and undermining.

Ethnicity

Although it is not always easily distinguishable from race, ethnicity is a distinct feature of school life. It includes not simply genetic makeup but also behavior patterns, values, and religious or national perspectives. It can be evident in speech patterns, particularly so when defining or clarifying is necessary in order to communicate. It includes notions of appropriate gender roles and of the hierarchy inherent in any given social interaction. Although ethnicity may be correlated with race, there also may be multiple ethnicities within the broad designation of a racial category.

Stephanie noted a pattern in some relationships between mothers and sons that she associated with Chinese families who had recently immigrated. She said:

> I don't understand some of the Chinese families, because it seems like the mothers bow down to their sons in a really deferential way. I think it is really unhealthy. I see their sons becoming real egomaniacs because they think they can do whatever they want. [For example, one mother said] *Oh I know,* [my son] *just walks all over me, and I don't know what to do.*

The dynamics of the students' families, often recently transplanted from dramatically different locales, perplexes Stephanie. The parents, like the students, are learning to negotiate a new country and culture, and the transition is often rocky. In at least this case, Stephanie does not view the cultural differences as benign. To the degree that this son is free to trounce his mother's authority at home, he may be likely to bridle all the more at Stephanie's attempts to exert control at school.

Immigrant parents have much to fear from the public school system and from public school teachers who may be oblivious to their own privileges as members of a majority culture. It is an alien world that their children must inhabit, with rules and expectations that may be literally or metaphorically incomprehensible. Unfortunately, this competitive dynamic pits the family's ways against the school's ways. As a result, sometimes defying a teacher becomes a measure of commitment and dedication to family or community. This kind of defiance also protects the student from

> ### Cultural Dynamics: Questioning Patterns
>
> Linguist Shirley Brice Heath found that conversation and questioning patterns vary according to culture. In research with white families, she found that parents used questions frequently to engage children as conversational partners. In contrast, among African American families, adults spoke to children primarily in imperatives. The children were unaccustomed to volunteering information, particularly rhetorical answers to questions. Likewise, white teachers often used commands phrased as questions ("Why don't you have a seat?"), which African American children, who were unfamiliar with these "indirect directives," ignored (Heath, 1982, p. 122). This variation in speech patterns, if unanticipated or misunderstood, can generate problems for students and teachers alike.

risk of failure following a sincere attempt at academic success. Poor marks in school can be attributed to lack of effort rather than lack of ability. To the degree that new teachers do not apprehend this dynamic, they unfairly may view deeply conflicted students or parents as uncooperative or antagonistic, underestimating the importance of saving face.

Helen described a recurring problem her first year with a boy who was destructive and disruptive. Initial parent contacts convinced Helen that the parents did not see the problems. One day, the boy deliberately ripped one of the large picture books that Helen had purchased with her own money for the classroom. She asked the boy's father, a recent immigrant from China, to attend a conference that afternoon where she proposed that they repair the book with tape. Instead, the father handed Helen twenty dollars and took the book. She explained:

> And I said, Well, you can't have the book. . . . Keep your money and what we need to do is just repair the book. And I took a very long time to carefully cut the tape and carefully have the little boy help me fix it while I was explaining to him that this is not all right and when we wreck things, we need to fix them. And the father could just barely stand to be in the room, and by the time the thing was over, he was very ready to go. And then I realized that he was basically losing face, and it was very uncomfortable for him.

The course of least resistance for Helen would have been to accept the money. However, money could not buy restitution so well as mending the book. Unfortunately, Helen also embarrassed the father by refusing his money and keeping him captive during the painstaking repair. Profound differences in ethnicity exacerbated the tension in this situation. Helen got the father's attention, but surely at some cost.

Paula tended to be less direct, and that approach has disadvantages, as well. She observed, "My nature is to be kind and polite and caring and nurturing to kids." Her notion of politeness included gentle requests, soft reminders, some cajoling, and when necessary, expressions of disappointment and hurt. One day, when a class relentlessly had given her a hard time, their regular teacher, an older African American woman, entered the room. Right away, she began pounding the palm of her hand on a desk. She got the students' attention immediately, and they were suddenly attentive and submissive. This teacher's style was no-nonsense, loud, dramatic, and undeniably effective at that moment. Paula's whole orientation as a teacher is different. Her notion of what it means to be polite and nurturing precludes this kind of tactic. Furthermore, had she attempted to mimic her colleague's trick, she might have found that it was perceived by some students as offensive. The context of ethnicity alters the interaction.

Similarly, Beth found great variations among students' speech patterns, and the differences sometimes made her uneasy. Specifically, she said:

> I find that my African American students often respond more to straightforward orders (as in "Darrell, sit down" vs. "Darrell, please sit down"); an African American teacher told me early on that this is how I should speak to African American students because that's how they're spoken to at home. She said that if I say, "Please," I lose some of my authority. I don't necessarily agree with her fully, but I have noticed that many of my African American students are used to being spoken to quite directly.

For new teachers who are white, this observation leads to some quandaries. This kind of straight talk may not feel comfortable or appropriate to them. Straight talk from a white teacher directed at a classroom of diverse students could be construed as demeaning, impolite, or disrespectful.

Karen noted that speech patterns created problems in communicating content, as well. She found that she was uncomfortable "delivering bad news" to parents. Believing that the parents of her students were often overwhelmed, she tried to soften any bad news and surround it with compliments. She was frustrated, however, that parents sometimes only seemed to hear the good news. Alternately, when the parents did hear the bad news, Karen felt that they became angry with her. Sometimes they would assume a protective stance and defend their children.

Karen's desire to soften her messages to parents may be partly attributed to ethnicity and partly to gender. Her impulse to pad the bad news with good is a strategy common to some women (Tannen, 1994), and her faith that the bad news will be communicated nonetheless is based on a cul-

Cultural Dynamics: Incompatible Worlds

In his research in Harlem, sociologist Philippe Bourgois found that cultural differences were profound when young male high school dropouts from the barrio took entry-level service jobs in the office buildings of Manhattan. Distinguishing direct orders from general guidelines proved difficult in this alien environment, and their attempts at initiative were interpreted by supervisors as an unwillingness or inability to follow explicit directions. Compounding the matter of weak professional skills, according to Bourgois, these young men "do not know how to look at their fellow service workers—let alone their supervisors—without intimidating them" (1995, p. 142). The skills of the street and the skills of the office were not only different, they were fundamentally incompatible. Culture-based miscommunication and misunderstanding of words, actions, and appearances can lead to problems, especially when these differences play out in a negative symbiosis with notions of gender.

tural understanding of the interplay between praise and reproof. In practice, however, her strategy obscures the most important part of the message. Any linguistic differences may lead Karen to heap on even more obfuscating praise in an effort to communicate her goodwill and affection for the child from a background unlike her own. However, pity the poor parent, native-born or immigrant, who tries to interpret what the teacher is saying. While someone fluent in the teacher's rhetorical niceties may understand the logic of spending the majority of the conversation generating goodwill in order to deliver bad news considerately, someone unfamiliar with this convention might mistake the spoonful of sugar for the medicine. Further, if it becomes clear, somehow, that there are serious problems in spite of the lengthy assurances, the parent might feel justifiably angry or at least wary of this teacher who does not seem to say what she means. Karen's efforts to be polite, respectful, and affirming end up generating ill will, confusion, and mistrust. This kind of exchange may reinforce parents' impression that the teacher is unable to relate to their child, or worse, willfully is withholding from the child vital information required for school success.

Finally, ethnicity includes incongruent notions of gender. White middle-class American women may think that equality of opportunity for males and females is a birthright. Few American women would argue that their society has created true parity, but most would concede that significant improvement has occurred in the past few decades. Women now in their twenties may take for granted extensive opportunities and legal recourse for discrimination. They may have grown up in settings where

Gender Dynamics: Bicultural Worlds

Each culture construes gender roles in distinct ways and with different means of monitoring and enforcing them. In Philippe Bourgois's research on male barrio residents working in Manhattan, "The machismo of street culture exacerbates the sense of insult experienced by men because the majority of office supervisors at the entry level are women," and there is a "street taboo against public male subordination to a woman" (Bourgois, 1995, p. 146). Nonetheless, these entry-level employees "are brusquely ordered about by young white executives—often female—who sometimes make bimonthly salaries superior to their underlings' yearly wages" (p. 147). Success in these jobs "requires an inner-city office worker to be bicultural: in other words, to play politely by 'the white woman's rules' downtown only to come home and revert to street culture within the safety of a tenement or housing project at night" (p. 170).

While the culture of schools is somewhat different than the culture of Manhattan offices, the gender dynamics may be similar. Many of the teachers—the first-line supervisors of students—are women, often young and white. While their salaries are modest by the standards of the business world, they may be greater than the household incomes of many of their students' families. Similarly, success in schools requires a certain bicultural facility. Urban students, especially those from immigrant or lower-class backgrounds, may find that the white middle-class ethos of schools is foreign. Their degree of success in negotiating one culture may impede their success in the other. These students face painful choices or bifurcated lives that their white middle-class peers may not confront.

equality for women was, if not a well-established community value, at least publicly espoused. Young white women from middle-class backgrounds may be unprepared for the fact that in some contexts, the notion of gender equity is still contested. In some cultures, gender equity may be experienced by a man as a "dramatic assault on his sense of masculine dignity" (Bourgois, 1995, p. 215). When notions of gender are contested, as they are likely to be in urban schools with diverse cultures, the difficulties of communication, discipline, and authority are compounded.

Class

Although it may be less overt than race or ethnicity, class is a very important factor in analyzing diversity. It can cross racial and ethnic boundaries. With the exception of Julie's school, which is atypical of the district, the other schools are characterized by urban, big-city features. Sociologist William Julius Wilson explained, "The central cities are becoming increasingly the domain of the poor and the stable working class" and are characterized by relatively high crime rates, significant numbers of female-headed households, and unemployment (Wilson, 1987, p. 136, p. 12). These matters affect schools. Jean Anyon, an educational researcher, found that social class influenced the character of schools in terms of curriculum and pedagogy. Working-class schools were more autocratic, while "affluent professional" schools emphasized greater choice, opportunity for negotiation, independent work, and autonomy (Anyon, 1988, p. 378). Compounding this difference, students in autocratic schools learned resistance, not obedience, further constraining teachers' choices. Meanwhile, students in more autonomous settings found greater satisfaction in school and invested more in it, expanding their teachers' curricular and pedagogical options. Administrative practices may reflect a similar pattern.

Given that teaching is middle-class work and schools have a middle-class ethos (Sikes, 1997), it might be tempting to assume that teachers from middle-class backgrounds relate best to students and parents from similar class backgrounds. In fact, the fickle chemistry of race, ethnicity, and class may make for unpredictable outcomes. For example, Stephanie recounted a conference with a girl in her class, Jamila, and her aunt. According to Stephanie, Jamila's mother was addicted to drugs, and Jamila lived with her aunt and grandmother who were functioning as her guardians. The purpose of the conference was to convey Jamila's significant academic and behavioral improvement to her aunt. Stephanie said, "I sat with her aunt for a little while this morning, and she kept saying, 'Thank you, Jesus! Thank you, Jesus!'" After giving Stephanie a big hug, the aunt "was just so happy, she looked like she was going to cry." For Stephanie, this kind of affirmation and appreciation "doesn't happen very often," and "it was really nice."

In contrast, Stephanie came to loggerheads with another parent, Angelique's mother. With a job at Kaiser Permanente, this mother had a steady income and benefits that were, if not middle-class, at least far closer to Stephanie's own situation than Jamila's mother. However, Stephanie reported, "I found that people who have it more together tend to give me a harder time." Specifically, Angelique's mother made demands that Stephanie found unreasonable:

> [The mother] called and said she wanted a progress report for Angelique. And I called back and said, "What do you mean 'a progress report?'" And she said, "Well, at my last school, all [I] had to do was ask for a progress report and I got one." And I said, "We don't have a form for progress reports, but if you want to come in and have a conference, I would be happy to talk to you about how

---

Cultural Dynamics: The Need for Diversity

The need for greater diversity among America's teaching professionals is acute. The young, white, middle-class women in this study felt the limitations of their own life experiences in preparing them to work with urban children.

Beth reported that an African American student told her, "I *really* wanted a black teacher this year." Initially, Beth thought, "Aren't I good enough?" Paula struggled with her sense that "a lot of [her] students would have been better served if they had had an African American teacher." Karen reported that one of her teacher education classmates told her, "You can't teach African American students. They'll never respect you."

Along with these African American students, Native American, Latino, Middle Eastern, Asian, Pacific Islander, and other children may hope to find themselves in a classroom with a teacher who looks like them. Our schools will be improved if these children are not disappointed year after year. Until that time, Paula noted wistfully, "I'm the one who's there. I'm the one they hired."

---

she is doing." She said, "No, I want a progress report. I want a written progress report."

Eventually, Stephanie wrote this mother a two-page report, although not before the mother had written a reminder note that Stephanie interpreted as a reproach. Stephanie's version of these events raises interesting questions about social class. If Jamila's mother really is addicted to drugs, and if the involvement of the aunt and grandmother suggest that no father is present, the household income of Jamila's nuclear family is likely to be dismally low. In contrast, Angelique's mother has a steady job with a major employer in the area. She clearly views her daughter's education as important, but she wants it on her terms, and Stephanie is put off by her specific and inconvenient requests. Arguably, Stephanie may be more comfortable interacting with appreciative poor families than with families in less dire straits who expect to have genuine input or want to complain.

Whether a new teacher believes that race, ethnicity, and social class should be irrelevant because they are subordinate to merit or because a caring teacher sees beyond them, she is likely to encounter conflicting viewpoints and evidence. In contrast, new teachers who believe that race, ethnicity, and class are central to the educational endeavor may find that they are paralyzed by the need to meet standards that are both high and nondiscriminatory, and by the conflicting demands of equity in opportunity and equity in outcome.

CONCLUSION

In a diverse setting, already-complex choices about curriculum and pedagogy become even more tangled. Every choice has a weak flank. For example, a teacher who emphasizes basic skills can be perceived as not providing a rich, theme-centered program for students. A teacher who prepares an extensive unit on ancient Greece may seem neglectful of students' current interests or inattentive to the contributions of diverse cultures. A teacher who demands that each student demonstrate a given mathematics proficiency before being promoted may seem unrealistic or rigid or exclusionary. A teacher who emphasizes the process of writing or fluency may be accused of abdicating responsibility for teaching basic literacy skills. A teacher who expects that significant work be completed outside of class time may be perceived as insensitive to the family responsibilities or housing situations of some students. Of course, few curriculum choices exist in isolation, and the context of the full year matters. Nonetheless, no choice is impervious to criticism.

For new teachers, especially, the opportunities for self-doubt and recrimination appear endless. If a teacher assumes that she should set a high standard and hold all students to it, is she setting up some of her neediest students for failure by pretending that they have an equal chance to meet it? If she sets a modest standard, is she underestimating the students and failing to challenge them? If she sets a variable standard, is she being fair? The teacher's best intentions may be rejected as flat-out wrong or, worse, malicious.

Intentions matter. Even in situations where there is no clear moral choice, where each action generates some guilt or loss or even harm, it is intentions that distinguish moral behavior from other pursuits. However, intentions have limits. The fact that they begin in good wishes does not necessarily imply that their results will be salutary. Intentions, conceived in isolation or within a single cultural context, may be inappropriate, harmful, or self-serving. To be beneficial, they must at least be guided by ethics, which Madeleine Grumet defines as "the discovery of those principles that can guide the moral conduct of persons who do not know each other" (1988, p. 167). Teachers and students must come to know one another, including their racial, ethnic, and class differences that are so persistently salient in classrooms across America.

9 Classrooms of Their Own

The luckiest new teachers enter classrooms of their own. Many of them are women, often young, often white. Others are male. Some are African American, Latino, Asian, Middle Eastern, or Native American. Some are beginning second careers. Others are returning to teaching after a hiatus at home or in another field. They carry into their classrooms a great variety of linguistic, political, and social sensibilities. Many, but not all, have middle-class backgrounds. They are this nation's new teachers.

Whether teachers literally have classrooms of their own or not, they must create for themselves and their students a sense of place. Both teacher and students need a sense of belonging in a classroom. They need a degree of comfort and familiarity and ownership. For the students, that comfort includes feeling accepted, valued, and guided toward educational attainment. For the teacher, this comfort includes a sense of competence.

Competence is not mastery. It is a preliminary and necessary step toward mastery. One of its by-products is enough hope and satisfaction to keep teaching, even in the face of other possible discouragements. Regardless of background, all new teachers must develop—through preservice preparation, inservice training, and on-the-job experience—at least preliminary levels of instructional, professional, and cultural competence.

INSTRUCTIONAL COMPETENCE

Like other professionals, most new teachers are less than proficient right out of the teacher education chute. Their legs wobble when they try to stand, and they will stagger about at first as they develop some strength and control. Painfully aware of their frailty, some involuntarily will make them-

Tips for New Teachers: Cultivating Instructional Competence

1. Make mistakes once only. Consciously analyze unsuccessful lessons or activities and make adjustments.

2. Take notes. Assume that your memory is fallible and provide yourself a written note (on a full-size sheet of paper in a logical place that you could locate again) about instructional successes and failures. Even a sticky note slapped on a lesson plan can be invaluable.

3. If possible, try to teach the same class or grade level more than once. Repetition will help control the variables and make it easier to identify your mistakes and successes.

4. Stay connected. Read professional journals, attend conferences, observe peers, and attend summer institutes as often as possible.

5. As part of your lesson planning process, be sure you can answer the following questions:

    • How does today's material relate to yesterday's and tomorrow's?

    • How am I going to interest students in this subject?

    • What is it that students should understand or be able to do after today's lesson?

    • How will I know what they have learned?

selves targets for others' aggression or sport. Others may imagine that since they are upright, they should try to run, leading to predictable spills.

Many new teachers are well aware of their own limited competence. Even as new teachers develop greater skill, they may not perceive their growth, particularly absent independent validation. The primacy many women place on external feedback is frustrated in teaching, where evaluation may be infrequent and is often perfunctory. As a result, while it is appropriate for new teachers to be mindful of their limited proficiency, they need not dwell on it unnecessarily.

Other new teachers may put too much faith in a credential. Since teacher certification is binary—one has it or one doesn't—it erases fine gradations. It is easy to believe that a teacher who has earned a certificate is, therefore, competent. It is then a simple skip from there to the assumption that a teacher who is competent is also skilled. New teachers who work for two or three years in the same district and avoid major blemishes on their records are more than likely to achieve tenure status. They may be only in

---

Age Dynamics: Youth and Idealism

Idealism is a hallmark of youth. A new teacher's fresh eyes may be a faculty's best hope for periodically reconsidering important matters that often go unexamined. Idealism conjures hope for a different and better world. Its advantages are clear: passion, vision, and commitment.

The disadvantages may be harder for a new teacher to perceive: ignorance of history, disregard for genuine impediments, and alienation and resentment from others whose efforts are overlooked or discounted. A balance of idealism and pragmatism can help young teachers work effectively within existing frameworks toward the goals they cherish.

---

their mid-twenties. If new teachers interpret the conferral of tenure as a personal affirmation rather than standard operating procedure, however, they misapprehend their competence.

Competence is essential for job satisfaction and professional retention. It is also necessary for achieving equity in public schools. Equitable school systems have a majority of competent teachers. Students are not shunted off to unproductive classrooms where their educational opportunities are squandered. As Hugh Sockett observed, "The primary way in which teachers, in their professional roles as members of a faculty, can create an equitable system is by working to the highest standards of which they are capable" (1993, p. 85). Content knowledge, pedagogy, and classroom organization and management are the foundations of these highest standards.

PROFESSIONAL COMPETENCE

Professional competence begins with realistic expectations about what teachers should do, can do, and are wise not to do. Unrealistic expectations lead to disappointment at best, and at worst, bitterness. Teaching is about helping people and making a difference in young lives. However, if a vision of teaching does not include taking attendance, reading countless scrawled compositions, selling popcorn at athletic events, punishing recalcitrants, justifying curriculum or grades to parents, and constantly trading off the needs of demanding students against their less aggressive classmates, then it is incomplete. At the K–12 levels, teaching is not a series of contemplative moments helping appreciative individuals far from the madding crowd; more often, it is a barrage of group encounters requiring spontaneous

Gender Dynamics: Women and Expectations

Women may be trained to be nice, to be peacemakers, to feel responsible for others' emotions, or to resolve problems in mutually satisfactory ways so that no one has hurt feelings or residual anger (Gilligan, 1982; McDonald & Rogers, 1995). These skills are valuable, and those who are proficient in them often enrich and enhance their institutions.

Nonetheless, absent other negotiation and management proficiency, this interpersonal orientation can be surprisingly harmful. Some women's socialization may set them up to want to do the impossible and then feel guilty when they fail. If two children are quarreling over a toy, a teacher can suggest taking turns as an approximate means of satisfying both. However, when competing groups of parents lobby for conflicting curricula, evaluation methods, priorities, or budgets, taking turns does not work. In fact, strategies that attempt to please all parties point to the weakest kind of compromise, lacking coherence and integrity. It is better in such cases—deliberately and thoughtfully—to disappoint somebody. In focusing on pleasant and mutually agreeable outcomes, the expectations of some women can be poor preparation for coming to terms with the conflicts inevitable in schools.

actions and frantic judgments that must stand up to scrutiny later. To imagine otherwise is to be misinformed.

New teachers who suppose that the world is out of order for no good reason and assume that they can fix it quickly are ignorant of their own ignorance. Given enough rope, they will hang themselves earnestly. Professional competence requires educating oneself about what has gone on before and why and how. Professional courtesy invites appreciation for the efforts of others and acknowledgment that learning to teach is a personal and collective evolution.

Professional competence includes a realistic view of a teacher's role. New teachers may underestimate the difficulty of creating tailor-made curricula and find themselves throwing together activities or borrowing prefabricated materials to fill class time. New teachers may imagine that their high expectations will inspire student success, forgetting that ultimately, students have agency. New teachers may believe that they can help all students develop the skills necessary to partake of middle-class economic rewards only to find that they can be perceived as obtuse or insensitive minions of institutional culture.

Finally, professional competence requires coming to terms with what it means to be in a helping profession. If the teacher imagines herself bestowing expertise on the less fortunate, she may drift into patronizing behavior that induces resentment and mistrust. Further, there may be a mismatch between enduring student needs and an idealistic teacher's periodic bouts of compassion. While infrequent episodes can be rejuvenating, full-time compassion is deeply wearying. The new teacher's expectation of correctly identifying needs, discerning and effecting appropriate responses, sustaining effort, and making a noticeable difference may go unfulfilled. The situations may be more complex, the requisite energy more difficult to maintain, and the results more ambiguous than some new teachers anticipate.

Professional competence entails a clear-eyed understanding of the job accompanied by focused and purposeful efforts to make that role rewarding and meaningful for both teacher and students. Professionalism is not the course of least resistance. It requires time, energy, planning, and risk. For some, this price may seem high. However, the price of not conducting one's work life like a professional is also high. In addition to greater isolation, decreased status and credibility, and fewer long-term options, unprofessional behavior diminishes authority. New teachers who would be effective must consider that trade-off carefully.

CULTURAL COMPETENCE

Finally, there is culture. New teachers must be prepared to work successfully with students from diverse backgrounds. A new teacher cannot become fully competent without an awareness, sensitivity, and appreciation for the cultures of the students she teaches.

On a philosophical level, this kind of cultural competence is important because it is the foundation of inclusive teaching. Inclusive teaching allows for students from different racial, ethnic, and social class backgrounds to assemble in public school classrooms across America. They can learn to read and write and solve equations, but they can also learn to listen and understand and build consensus. They can learn to disagree and to work together anyway. They can learn to respect other people and other ways of thinking.

Inclusive teaching is also a practical strategy. It creates environments in which students can feel accepted, engaged, and safe. They are free from some of the distractions that can impede learning. They may become invested in the classroom community and more responsive to their teacher. As they sense her interest in them as individuals and her commitment to maximizing their future opportunities, they are more likely to cooperate and do their best work. They may be motivated by a curriculum that seems relevant and interesting to them. They may feel that the teacher understands and appreciates them, and believe that effort and diligence—rather than bias or bigotry—will determine their degree of success.

Cultural Dynamics: Inclusive Teaching

- Treat students as individuals, not as representatives of racial, ethnic, or social class groups to which they may belong.

- Remember that any large group has tremendous variation within it. It is fair to ask students to speak as individuals; it is not fair to ask them to speak for a whole group.

- Stop instruction to respond if students make comments that are prejudiced, discriminatory, or hurtful.

- Establish guidelines for discussion that allow disagreement based on evidence or sound information. Do not allow personal attacks.

- Make the class content reflect the different racial, ethnic, and social class backgrounds of the students and the larger community. Throughout the year, try to integrate this content in meaningful ways that avoid stereotypes. Toward that end, invite parents or other guests, include readings, show films, attend concerts or museums, display art, taste cuisine, discuss current events, or in other ways explore the cultural diversity of the class.

This kind of inclusive classroom is not easy to achieve. However, it is nearly impossible to achieve if the teacher lacks cultural competence. It is the teacher who bears much of the responsibility for creating such an environment. It is she who determines structures and processes, rewards and formal interactions. For new teachers, struggling to master new curriculum, gain facility with pedagogical techniques, learn names, figure out how to get needed support around school, and still get some sleep, cultural competence may seem like a nicety for some future time. It is not. It is essential from the first day, and new teachers who would be authoritative in the eyes of all their students and parents must attend to it.

PRACTICAL CONSIDERATIONS

It is in the best interests of schools everywhere—not to mention the students, parents, teachers, communities, and nations they serve—to facilitate the creation of a teaching force that is engaged and energized by its work. Before teachers can be free to rethink practices, modify the culture of schools, or work cooperatively to implement change, they must be free from oppressive or unfair work demands and the resulting personal duress. Teaching has been described as the "profession that eats its young"

Cultural Dynamics: Equitable Class Discussions

It is easy for a few vocal students to monopolize discussion time and for quiet or unprepared students to become passive listeners. Race, ethnicity, class, and gender often influence the roles students assume during discussions. Teachers can help all students by providing specific information about what students can expect and how they might prepare. Here are a few strategies for fostering equitable discussions:

Preparation

- Announce the subject and format of a discussion in advance so that students can prepare. Privately let individual students know that they should be prepared to participate.

- Advertise the length of wait time to focus student attention. ("In 90 seconds, I'll call on three people to respond.")

- In lieu of wait time, provide prediscussion activities such as journal writing or brainstorming with a partner.

- Ask questions in a sequence from easier to harder, with fact-based questions first.

- Offer quiet students first crack at some easy, low-risk questions.

- Have students vote on a continuum to establish relative positions. ("Was Charlotte's decision defensible? On a scale of 1 to 10, what number best describes your feelings?") Use this information to gauge changes in student positions and to draw out differing opinions. ("Maria, you were a 2. Can you tell us why?")

Respondents

- Use volunteers sparingly. ("Please put your hands down now.") Ask a question, provide wait time, and then call on someone. Or use a random method such as dice, a spinner, names in a jar, last names from A to H, students wearing red shirts, and so on.

- Narrow the pool of possible respondents. ("I'd like to hear from someone who hasn't spoken yet." "Can we hear from someone who disagrees with Ben?" "Let's hear opinions from everyone in row four.")

- Strive for diversity of respondents. Try alternating between boys and girls. Be sure to call on students from different racial, ethnic, or class backgrounds. As well, call on students from all parts of the room, especially back rows and corners.

Continued

Note Taking

- If possible, use a student scribe to write discussion notes on the board so that you can face the speaker, scan the room, and plan your next move.

- Devise visual or graphic representations to help students take notes on discussions and to organize their thoughts (charts, maps, graphs, Venn diagrams, timelines, etc.). Ask students to copy from the board or else distribute a note-taking handout.

- Try to copy students' comments verbatim. Avoid the temptation to translate their words into your own, unless the meaning is completely unclear. When student comments must be edited for brevity, ask the student to pare them down. ("How shall I write that? Does this phrase say what you mean?")

Overall

- Hear every voice, literally. Insist on quiet, respectful listening. If possible, when you call on a student, move as far away from him as possible to encourage projection and enunciation. If a student mumbles, ask her to repeat herself instead of paraphrasing her remarks.

- For purposes of sustaining discussion, use affirmative responses that encourage additional comments. ("Yes. Other thoughts?" "Thank you. That's an important point. Who can build on that idea?" "I'm glad you brought that subject up. Javon, Anne, and Felipe, could each of you please react to this idea?") Minimize the use of absolute words such as "right" or "correct" since they tend to stifle other comments and bring closure that may be premature.

- Call home and praise lavishly when a student makes an important or uncharacteristic contribution to a discussion.

(Halford, 1998, p. 33). Many of those young are women, and it is their early afflictions that are so often mortal. Making schools feasible places for all new teachers to work is an essential component of meaningful reform.

Ironically, while the situation is complex, the first-line remedies are not. Teacher educators can alter existing curricula to include greater attention to the opportunities and constraints of gender and age as part of a primer of organizational literacy that is specific to schools. They can make explicit the range of strategies for enhancing personal and institutional authority. Teacher educators can be candid about the tension between exposing new teachers to strategies that could be transformative in the long run but likely to exact a high toll in the short run. For example, pedagogy designed to give students greater control of their education, whether cooperative learning, student portfolios, workshop-style writing programs, or self-paced/self-assessed work, may be innovative and effective means of instruction. In the hands of novices, however, they can lead to problems with authority, perhaps particularly for new teachers. When well-meaning teacher educators try to effect school change by urging novices to attempt complex and sophisticated pedagogies, they inadvertently may set up those teachers for failure. Under those circumstances, the division between what is properly teacher preservice education and what is properly inservice or professional development is ill conceived.

As well, administrators must make appropriate assignments and allocate resources fairly. Appropriate assignments for new teachers will have a minimal number of changing variables such as subject matter, grade level, ability level, room assignment, texts and materials, instructional aides, extracurricular responsibilities, and students. Some variables are inevitable and may be desirable. However, too many variables are overwhelming, add layers of logistical complexity to new and demanding responsibilities, and make isolating problems difficult. Supportive administrators can help monitor fairness and reasonability for new teachers by advocating formal rather than informal procedures for distributing resources. To the degree that these processes are made explicit, new teachers are better situated to work effectively.

In addition, administrators must support new teachers actively. Administrators and colleagues can offer no greater support than publicly endorsing new teachers' actions. There may be a need for private discussions and mentoring, and in extreme cases, termination, but in general, dependable public support is the most valuable offering administrators can tender new teachers. Mindful of the multiplier effect that compounds the status deficit of a new employee with any status deficits associated with age, gender, race, ethnicity, or class, administrators can help compensate with unambiguous and consistent support. They can make sure that institutional authority means something.

Creating Fewer Vacancies

Teaching vacancies are likely to plague many schools in the next decade. Some of the vacancies are caused by retirement, but many are the result of new teachers quitting in the first three to five years of their careers (National Commission, 2001). In the often-difficult circumstances of schools, new teachers bear much of the compression, and their discomfort, discontent, and discouragement leave one-way tracks heading out.

Tips for Administrators and Mentors: Supporting New Teachers

- In addition to handbooks, curriculum guides, and phone lists, provide meaningful and ongoing orientation regarding both formal and informal policies and practices. ("How do evaluations really work?" "What is a realistic discipline procedure at this school?" "To whom can I turn for help?")

- Make sure new teachers get their fair share of available resources. Ask what they need and try to help them procure it.

- If at all possible, provide new teachers with classrooms of their own. If they must travel, minimize the number of rooms and distances between them.

- Stop by new teachers' classrooms frequently during the first few months.

- Seek out informal conversations.

- Provide specific evaluative feedback early and often.

- Advocate for them with parents and administrators. Make sure the new teachers know about your efforts.

- Praise them. Encourage them. Give them reason to feel known and valued.

For young women, there may be special and aggravating considerations about the viability of a teaching career. If the working conditions make a woman feel unsafe, she may want to make a change in order to preserve her own sense of comfort. If her teaching assignment and schedule create an unworkable situation in which she has undue management problems, she may experience greater professional stress and anxiety than some male colleagues (Calabrese & Anderson, 1986; Hochschild, 1989; Martin, 1990; Robertson, 1992). In addition, if the conditions of teaching make a new teacher feel isolated in decrepit facilities with chalk-dusty clothes and runny noses, they may diminish her career satisfaction. Finally, if the expected rewards of teaching evolve into dependence on uncooperative children or indifferent colleagues for the accomplishment of self-worth, new teachers, especially women, may be particularly prone to feelings of powerlessness. Taken together, these factors can create a mood of uncertainty that may make teachers reluctant to engage themselves fully in their work. Consequently, they may be less effective and derive fewer rewards.

In stemming the exodus of new teachers from classrooms around the country, the importance of having a group of experienced, mature teachers on any given faculty is clear. These teachers, the seasoned veterans who have figured out ways to function successfully and with satisfaction in schools, are an absolutely essential resource. They are also surprisingly rare. When turnover is high, faculties can become collections of newcomers of varying degrees with little grasp of institutional history and little professional experience or expertise among them. It is difficult to provide mentors, make coherent policies that are likely to be carried out, or develop positive ongoing relationships with district administrators or families under these circumstances. There are few teachers with enough control over their professional lives to be attentive to the needs of new people. There are few role models demonstrating the rewards of a career in teaching.

There is an urgent need to attract more—and more diverse—teachers for our nation's schools. There is no substitute for a teaching pool that reflects the diversity of the citizens it serves.

However, the easiest way to attract new teachers is to retain the current ones. This process requires supporting them in becoming instructionally, professionally, and culturally competent so that they can be effective. It is to ensure that their working conditions are workable. It is to make teaching rewarding and feasible for new teachers, including the majority who are young women.

Simple Matters

At one level, the experience of new teachers is fairly simple. Frequently, they are inexperienced, the situation is deceptively complex, they make mistakes, little help is forthcoming, and they get discouraged. Their discouragement is telling about the school environment. If their experience is fragmented, aggravating, superficial, hostile, or alienating, chances are that at least some students are encountering an environment at least as incompatible with intellectual growth, physical safety, and social or civic development. Such an environment matters. Whether the experience of new teachers leads to withdrawal from the profession, a bunker mentality in the classroom, or renewed commitment to more effective teaching, it reflects an experience that is often fundamentally discouraging.

Discouragement is not simple. According to Hugh Sockett, "Encouragement and discouragement are highly sophisticated moral acts, the purpose of which is both to get the children to learn whatever is to be learned and also to summon up their will" (1993, p. 74). Perhaps as much as any specific content, a dose of encouragement is vital to children's academic success. However, children are not the only ones in schools facing intimidating new situations. Adults are learners, too, and young adults in a new profession are likely to be learning at least as much as they are teaching.

Tips for New Teachers: Be Kind to Yourself

- Take at least a full day off from schoolwork every weekend. Limit the amount of time you spend on schoolwork over vacation breaks. You will resent your job if you allow it to stalk you during all your hours away.

- Give yourself credit for your students' successes. There may be many contributors, including parents, other teachers, and the students themselves, but give yourself due acknowledgment. You will get your share of blame—and more, sometimes—for problems and unfulfilled hopes, so be sure to savor the best moments.

- Have fun. Laugh out loud with your students. Make friends with your colleagues. Take an interest in the lives around you.

- Do something that has nothing to do with school. Do it even if you don't have time. Take tennis lessons. Join a choir. Volunteer in a religious, political, or community organization. Train your dog. Learn to cook. Form a book group. Take up woodworking. On days when you feel less than competent at school, you can still be competent in other places for other people doing other activities. Have a life in addition to a job.

Encouraging new teachers should mean literally putting courage into them to keep doing their demanding jobs, ideally with increasing skill and success.

This kind of encouragement finds form in organized and equitable processes, collegial dialogue, adequate materials, respect, administrative backing, and a sense of fairness that bolster a teacher, rather than in trite phrases of general good wishes. If the school halls, the faculty lounge, the office, the district administration building, and the classrooms are not places where the teacher finds this kind of routine support, no amount of verbal assurance will encourage her. Encouragement requires attention from others who have greater understanding and control of the circumstances of teaching. Teacher educators, colleagues, and administrators bear an essential charge in providing this kind of assistance as much as possible. As they consider the experience of new teachers, they may borrow from John Dewey and ask, "Does this form of growth create conditions for further growth, or does it set up conditions that shut off the person who has grown?" (Dewey, 1938, p. 36). The experiences of new teachers should not shut them off.

Unfamiliar situations are usually challenging and not everyone is suited to teaching, but ideally, turnover would not be the result of discouragement as much as of a more basic mismatch or incompatibility. Perhaps even more damaging than turnover is the teacher who shuts off in place, ineffectual and inert. In either case, discouraging experience stymies professional growth. The experience of students in schools should be educative, in Dewey's sense of fostering continued growth; new teachers deserve no less.

In Laura Ingalls Wilder's autobiographical books for children, the young Laura anticipates her first job as a teacher with some trepidation, while her father tries to encourage her:

> "Well, Laura! You are a schoolteacher now! We knew you would be, didn't we? Though we didn't expect it so soon."
>
> "Do you think I can, Pa?" Laura answered. "Suppose—just suppose—the children won't mind me when they see how little I am."
>
> "Of course you can," Pa answered. "You've never failed yet at anything you tried to do, have you?"
>
> "Well, no," Laura admitted. "But I—I never tried to teach school." (Wilder, 1943, pp. 2-3)

References

Acker, S. (1995). Gender and teachers' work. In M. W. Apple (Ed.), *Review of research in education* (pp. 99-162). Madison, WI: American Educational Research Association.

American Association of University Women Educational Foundation. (1992). *The AAUW report: How schools shortchange girls.* Washington, DC: Author.

Anderson, S., Rolheiser, C., & Gordon, K. (1998). Preparing teachers to be leaders. *Educational Leadership, 55*(5), 59-61.

Anyon, J. (1988). Social class and the hidden curriculum of work. In J. R. Gress (Ed.), *Curriculum: An introduction to the field* (pp. 366-389). Berkeley, CA: McCutchan Publishing Corporation.

Barber, S. N., & Estrin, E. T. (1996). *Culturally responsive mathematics and science education for native students.* San Francisco: Far West Laboratory for Educational Research and Development.

Belenky, M. F., Clinchy, B. M., Goldberger, N. R., & Tarule, J. M. (1986). *Women's ways of knowing: The development of self, voice, and mind.* New York: Basic Books.

Biklen, S. K. (1993). Mothers' gaze from teachers' eyes. In S. K. Biklen & D. Pollard (Eds.), *Gender and education* (Vol. 92, pp. 155-173). Chicago: University of Chicago Press.

Biklen, S. K. (1995). *School work: Gender and the cultural construction of teaching.* New York: Teachers College Press.

Black, A., & Davern, L. (1998). When a preservice teacher meets the classroom team. *Educational Leadership, 55*(5), 52-54.

Bourdieu, P. (1986). The forms of capital. In J. G. Richardson (Ed.), *Handbook of theory and research for the sociology of education.* New York: Greenwood.

Bourgois, P. (1995). *In search of respect: Selling crack in El Barrio.* New York: Cambridge University Press.

Bowles, S., & Gintis, H. (1975). Capitalism and education in the United States. *Socialist Revolution, 5,* 101-138.

Brown, L. M., & Gilligan, C. (1992). *Meeting at the crossroads.* New York: Ballantine.

Bullough, R. V., Jr. (1989). *First-year teacher: A case study.* New York: Teachers College Press.

Calabrese, R. L., & Anderson, R. E. (1986). The public school: A source of stress and alienation among female teachers. *Urban Education, 21*(1), 30-41.

Cameron, D. (1994). Verbal hygiene for women: Linguistics misapplied? *Applied Linguistics, 15*(4), 382-398.

Clandinin, D. J., & Connelly, F. M. (1995). *Teachers' professional knowledge landscapes.* New York: Teachers College Press.

Connell, R. W. (1985). *Teachers' work.* Sydney, Australia: George Allen & Unwin.

Dee, T. S. (2001). *Teachers, race and student achievement in a randomized experiment.* National Bureau of Economic Research. Retrieved October 15, 2001, from http://www.nber.org

Delpit, L. (1995). *Other people's children: Cultural conflict in the classroom.* New York: New Press.

Dewey, J. (1938). *Experience and education.* New York: Collier Books.

Dilworth, M. E. (1990). *Reading between the lines: Teachers and their racial/ethnic cultures.* Washington, DC: U.S. Department of Education, Office of Educational Research and Improvement.

Dornbusch, S. M., Glasgow, K. L., & Lin, I.-C. (1996). The social structure of schooling. *Annual Review of Psychology, 47,* 401-429.

Dreeben, R. (1973). The school as a workplace. In R. M. W. Travers (Ed.), *Second handbook of research on teaching.* Chicago: Rand McNally.

England, P. (1992). *Comparable worth.* New York: Aldine De Gruyter.

Feistritzer, E. (1990). Profile of teachers in the U.S.—1990. Washington, DC: The National Center for Education Information.

Freire, P. (1970). *Pedagogy of the oppressed* (M. B. Ramos, Trans.). New York: Continuum.

Gardner, H. (1993). *Multiple intelligences: The theory in practice.* New York: Basic Books.

Gilligan, C. (1982). *In a different voice: Psychological theory and women's development.* Cambridge, MA: Harvard University Press.

Griffin, G. A. (1995). Influences of shared decision making on school and classroom activity: Conversations with five teachers. *The Elementary School Journal, 96*(1), 29-45.

Grumet, M. R. (1988). *Bitter milk: Women and teaching.* Amherst: University of Massachusetts Press.

Halford, J. M. (1998). Easing the way for new teachers. *Educational Leadership, 55*(5), 33-36.

Heath, S. B. (1982). Questioning at home and at school: A comparative study. In G. Spindler (Ed.), *Doing the ethnography of school* (pp. 102-131). New York: Holt, Rinehart and Winston.

Heller, M. F., & Firestone, W. A. (1995). Who's in charge here? Sources of leadership for change in eight schools. *The Elementary School Journal, 96*(1), 65-86.

Hochschild, A. R. (1989). *The second shift.* New York: Avon Books.

Hollinger, C. L., & Fleming, E. S. (1992). A longitudinal examination of life choices of gifted and talented young women. *Gifted Child Quarterly, 36*(4), 207-212.

Jencks, C. (1992). *Rethinking social policy.* Cambridge, MA: Harvard University Press.

Kanter, R. M. (1977). *Men and women of the corporation.* New York: Basic Books.

Kozol, J. (1991). *Savage inequalities: Children in America's schools.* New York: Crown Publishers.

Labbett, B. (1988). Skilful neglect. In J. Schostak (Ed.), *Breaking into the curriculum* (pp. 89-104). London: Methuen.

Ladson-Billings, G. (1994). *The dreamkeepers: Successful teachers of African American children*. San Francisco: Jossey-Bass.

Licht, B. G. (1987, April). *The interaction between children's achievement-related beliefs and the characteristics of different tasks.* Paper presented at the annual meeting of the American Educational Research Association, Washington, DC.

Lightfoot, S. L. (1983). *The good high school*. New York: Basic Books.

Lindblad, S., & Prieto, H. P. (1992). School experiences and teacher socialization: A longitudinal study of pupils who grew up to be teachers. *Teaching and Teacher Education, 8*(5/6), 465-470.

Lortie, D. (1975). *Schoolteacher: A sociological study.* Chicago: University of Chicago Press.

Magolda, M. B. B. (1995). The integration of relational and impersonal knowing in young adults' epistemological development. *Journal of College Student Development, 36*(3), 205-216.

March, J. G. (1988). Bounded rationality, ambiguity, and the engineering of choice. In J. G. March (Ed.), *Decisions and organizations* (pp. 587-608). Oxford: Blackwell.

Martin, J. (1994). The organization of exclusion: Institutionalization of sex inequality, gendered faculty jobs and gendered knowledge in organizational theory and research. *Organization, 1*(2), 401-431.

Martin, J. R. (1990). The contradiction of the educated woman. In J. Antler & S. K. Biklen (Eds.), *Changing education: Women as radicals and conservatives.* Albany: State University of New York Press.

McDonald, L., & Rogers, L. (1995, April). *Who waits for the white knight? Training in "nice."* Paper presented at the annual meeting of the American Educational Research Association, San Francisco.

McPherson, J. M., & Smith-Lovin, L. (1986). Sex segregation in voluntary associations. *American Sociological Review, 51*(February), 61-79.

McPherson, J. M., & Smith-Lovin, L. (1987). Homophily in voluntary associations: Status distance and the composition of face-to-face groups. *American Sociological Review, 52*(June), 370-379.

Measor, L. (1985). Critical incidents in the classroom: Identities, choices, and careers. In S. J. Ball & I. F. Goodson (Eds.), *Teachers' lives and careers* (pp. 61-77). London: Falmer.

Meek, A. (1998). America's teachers: Much to celebrate. *Educational Leadership, 55*(5), 12-16.

National Center for Education Statistics. (1996). *Schools and staffing in the United States: A statistical profile 1993-94.* Washington, DC: U.S. Department of Education, Office of Educational Research and Improvement.

National Center for Education Statistics. (2000). *Digest of education statistics, 2000.* Retrieved September 28, 2001, from nces.ed.gov/pubs2001/digest/

National Commission on Teaching and America's Future. (2001). Teachers College, Columbia University. Retrieved October 8, 2001, from http://www.tc.columbia.edu/nctaf/

Noddings, N. (1984). *Caring: A feminine approach to ethics and moral education.* Berkeley: University of California Press.

Nussbaum, M. C. (1990). *Love's knowledge: Essays on philosophy and literature* (pp. 54-105). New York: Oxford University Press.

Orenstein, P. (1994). *Schoolgirls: Young women, self-esteem, and the confidence gap.* Garden City, NY: Doubleday.

Paley, V. G. (1979). *White teacher.* Cambridge, MA: Harvard University Press.

Peshkin, A. (1988). In search of subjectivity—one's own. *Educational Researcher, 17*(7), 17-21.

Peshkin, A. (1992). Making words fly. In C. Glesne & A. Peshkin (Eds.), *Becoming a qualitative researcher.* New York: Longman.

Pfeffer, J., & Salancik, G. (1978). *The external control of organizations.* New York: Harper and Row.

Pipher, M. (1994). *Reviving Ophelia: Saving the selves of adolescent girls.* New York: Ballantine Books.

Recruiting New Teachers. (2001). *Teaching field facts.* Retrieved June 12, 2001, from http://www.rnt.org/facts/index.html

Reis, R. M. (1997). *Tomorrow's professor: Preparing for academic careers in science and engineering.* New York: Institute of Electrical and Electronics Engineers.

Robertson, H.-J. (1992). Teacher development and gender equity. In M. G. Fullan & A. Hargreaves (Eds.), *Understanding teacher development* (pp. 43-61). New York: Teachers College Press.

Rodriguez, R. (1982). *Hunger of memory: The education of Richard Rodriguez.* New York: Bantam Books.

Rose, M. (1989). *Lives on the boundary.* New York: Penguin.

Ruddick, S. (1980). Maternal thinking. *Feminist Studies, 6*(2), 342-367.

Schmidt, M., & Knowles, J. G. (1995). Four women's stories of "failure" as beginning teachers. *Teaching and Teacher Education, 11*(5), 429-444.

Sikes, P. (1997). *Parents who teach: Stories from home and from school.* New York: Cassell.

Sizer, T. R. (1984). *Horace's compromise.* Boston: Houghton Mifflin.

Smith, G. A. (1994). Preparing teachers to restructure schools. *Journal of Teacher Education, 45*(1), 18-30.

Sockett, H. (1993). *The moral base of teacher professionalism.* New York: Teachers College Press.

Tannen, D. (1990). *You just don't understand.* New York: William Morrow.

Tannen, D. (1994). *Talking from 9 to 5.* New York: Avon Books.

Webb, R. B. (1985). Teacher status panic: Moving up the down escalator. In S. J. Ball & I. F. Goodson (Eds.), *Teachers' lives and careers* (pp. 78-88). London: Falmer.

Weiner, L. (1993). *Preparing teachers for urban schools.* New York: Teachers College Press.

Wilder, L. I. (1943). *These happy golden years.* New York: Harper & Brothers.

Willower, D. J. (1969). The teacher subculture and rites of passage. *Urban Education, 4*(2), 103-114.

Wilson, J. Q., & Kelling, G. L. (1982, March). Broken windows. *Atlantic Monthly, 249*, 29-38.

Wilson, W. J. (1987). *The truly disadvantaged: The inner city, the underclass, and public policy.* Chicago: University of Chicago Press.

Yasin, S. (1999). *The supply and demand of elementary and secondary school teachers in the United States.* Retrieved September 28, 2001, from www.ed.gov/databases/ERIC_Digests/ed436529.html

Suggestions for Further Reading

Atkin, J. M. (1992). Teaching as research: An essay. *Teaching and Teacher Education, 8*(4), 381-390.

Bullough, R. (2001). *Uncertain lives: Children of promise, teachers of hope.* New York: Teachers College Press.

Cuban, L. (1988). *The managerial imperative and the practice of leadership in schools.* Albany: State University of New York Press.

Dilworth, M. E. (1998). *Being responsive to cultural differences: How teachers learn.* Thousand Oaks, CA: Corwin Press.

Eisner, E. W. (1991). *The enlightened eye: Qualitative inquiry and the enhancement of practice.* New York: Macmillan.

Howard, G. R. (1999). *We can't teach what we don't know: White teachers, multiracial schools.* New York: Teachers College Press.

Huberman, M. (1989). The professional life cycle of teachers. *Teachers College Record, 91*(1), 31-57.

Kuzmic, J. (1994). A beginning teacher's search for meaning: Teacher socialization, organizational literacy, and empowerment. *Teaching and Teacher Education, 10*(1), 15-27.

Maher, F. A., & Tetreault, M. K. T. (1994). *The feminist classroom.* New York: Basic Books.

Reiger, K. (1993). The gender dynamics of organizations: A historical account. In J. Blackmore & J. Kenway (Eds.), *Gender matters in educational administration and policy: A feminist introduction* (pp. 17-26). London: Falmer.

Ridgeway, C. L. (1993). Gender, status, and the social psychology of expectations. In P. England (Ed.), *Theory on gender/Feminism on theory* (pp. 175-197). New York: Aldine De Gruyter.

Thorne, B. (1995). *Gender play: Girls and boys in school.* New Brunswick, NJ: Rutgers University Press.

Weber, M. (1946). Bureaucracy. In H. Gerth & C. W. Mills (Eds.), *From Max Weber* (pp. 196-244). New York: Oxford University Press.

Weick, K. (1982). Administering education in loosely coupled schools. *Phi Delta Kappan, 63*(10), 673-676.

Index